UNTHINK
ALL YOU HAVE TO DO IS NOTHING

BY DR. ERIC ZABIEGALSKI

Cover design in collaboration with Shayna Zabiegalski, Artist.

Printed in the United States of America

ISBN 979-8-88955-556-8 Paperback

ISBN 979-8-88955-377-9 Ebook

"Building on his first breakthrough book, The *Rise of the Ambidextrous Organization*, Dr. Zabiegalski has written another exciting book! UNTHINK is about learning to ask questions with the curiosity we once had as children, to listen with new focus and awareness, and to act in the right kinds of ways. A natural companion to *The Rise of the AO*, this time Eric focuses on the individual instead of the organization, showing the reader how to easily achieve excellence at work and wisdom in life. By questioning traditional structures and traditional thinking, Eric teaches the reader how to lead and manage from ancient foundations of Indigenous peoples as well as the scientific principles and theories no one else talks about. Whether it's *storytelling* in a living world or practicing *proprioception of thought* for the muscle/organ in your head, Eric's book is bold and fresh. This book will help you distinguish *intuition* from *bias*, *memory* from real-time *awareness*, and *observation* from reflexive thought. In short, this book will help you 'UNTHINK'!"
—MICHAEL J. MARQUARDT
Professor Emeritus, George Washington University
Co-founder, World Institute for Action Learning
Author of 27 books in the fields of leadership, learning, globalization, and organizational change

"This is the right book for right now. Yes, thinking requires focus. But unthinking and rethinking requires much more—it requires choosing courage over comfort. Eric weaves together research and storytelling to help us build the intellectual and emotional muscle we need to stay curious enough about the world to actually change it. Cover to cover, Eric examines the critical art of unthinking: learning to question everything, opening your mind and perhaps the minds of people within the inner circle of your life, which can position you for excellence at work and wisdom in life. UNTHINK reveals that we don't have to believe everything we think or internalize everything we feel. It's an invitation to let go of views that are no longer serving us well and prize mental flexibility over foolish consistency. If knowledge is power, knowing what we don't

know and unthinking what we do know is wisdom. Eric kept his promise to take me on a journey and deliver me to a new destination, changed at the end of the final chapter. In other words, he accomplished the UNTHINKable."
—DENNIS J. PITOCCO
Publisher and Editor-in-Chief
Award-Winning BizCatalyst 360°

"Great read! Eric's work in *UNTHINK* maps an undiscovered intersection of ambidexterity, quantum, Indigenous, field theory, complexity, mindfulness, and a few other cutting-edge perspectives for improving both businesses and lives in general. He explains complex theories clearly. His illuminating stories from business and management, combined with his wealth of personal experiences using 'unthinking,' make it an understandable and ready-to-apply book."
—GRACE ANN ROSILE, PhD
Management Professor Emeritus, New Mexico State University
Editor of the book of collected readings *Tribal Wisdom for Business Ethics* (Emerald, 2016)

"*UNTHINK* by Dr. Eric Zabiegalski takes the reader on a journey of deeper understanding to navigate and prosper in a world where the speed of light is the speed of life. He does this not simply by sharing a breadcrumb trail, but by creating an illuminated path of examples, stories, and ideas to help us evolve, as individuals and organizations, becoming more *involved* in the way we think, feel, and act. This book shows us how to be more innovative, curious, and mentally unstuck in a world that requires it more often. Though his ideas are complex, the book is accessible, practical, and entertaining. We need better, different approaches to solve today's problems, and *UNTHINK* provides a powerful lens to do it!"
—D. J. VANAS (Ottawa Tribe)
Speaker and author of *The Warrior Within* (Penguin Random House)
Host of the PBS Special *Discovering Your Warrior Spirit*

"*Unthink* is a masterfully comprehensive presentation of Western and Indigenous strategies for understanding and organizing your

thoughts and ideas and transforming them into pragmatic leadership activity."
—JOSEPH SCOTT (JOE) GLADSTONE, PhD
Business Management Professor, Indigenous & Community Business Education Development, Washington State University

"There's a vision beyond the sighted world that's difficult to achieve; sadly, many never get there. This vision shines with a light as bright and warm as a New Mexico sun, sees with the sharpness of a hawk, and imagines with a pallet as colorful as a tropical sea. It's the vision of pure awareness and gives voice (and vision) to intuition, creativity, imagination, and the wisdom of the sub-conscious. It's my wish for *everyone* to see with that vision, achieve that indomitable spirit, and live their very best lives. You can get there, through struggle, challenge, chance, or fate, and hope for the best, or you can learn to UNTHINK. Bravo, Dr. Zabiegalski."
—GEORGE MENDOZA
Artist and Visionary

"UNTHINK is a bold invitation designed to return us to our roots, our collective humanity by sharing and evolving our true stories. Dr. Zabiegalski deftly integrates tips for restoring yourself and your workplace by instilling culture, connection, compassion, and kindness with vigorously researched theoretical knowledge providing a deeper understanding of how and why true storytelling works for business. This isn't pie-in-the-sky but real-world practices you can apply to help move humanity forward. UNTHINK is a clarion call to all those with a keen desire to learn how to 'architect a better world for everyone to live and work in.' If this is you, join us to better the world for good."
—DIANE F. WYZGA, RN, JD
Founder, Engaged Storyism Method

"*A Clockwork Orange* is a classic dystopian movie about the role of thinking and programming as they shape our behavior. The central character, Alex, a brilliant but violent gang member, is sat in front of a screen showing violence and sexual content, his eyes held open, until his physical and sexual aggression is gone. They both come

back. Our brains have remarkable resilience, flexibility . . . and stubbornness. The last of these snaps us back to old pathways regardless of their appropriateness. To move away from Alex's world of a very disturbing future, how can we better think? What if we're looking at it backwards —we have to better unthink. *Unthink: All You Have To Do Is Nothing* grabbed me with its wide-ranging scope—stimulation, humility, the pandemic, storytelling, 'the arrogance of ignorance,' and my favorite, the Memory Palace. And within this complex journey, Eric returns to a simple theme: before we can change *what* we think, we must change *how* we think, and *Unthink* walks us—runs us, really—to the way there."
—MAC BOGERT
President, AzaLearning

"A remarkable book that explores ideas that will aid leaders at all levels by showing the benefits of leveraging both their right and left-brain hemispheres. Through an absorbing narrative, Dr. Eric Zabiegalski reveals how exploiting the power of intuition, and leveraging process-based decision-making, can empower organizations, improving innovation, avoiding cognitive bias, removing organization inertia, etc. An essential read for leaders facing volatility, ambiguity, complexity, uncertainty so prevalent within the post-industrial era."
—J. SCOTT "SCOOTER" O'MEARA
Brigadier General, U.S. Marine Corps, Retired

"Very insightful! The book UNTHINK written by Dr. Eric Zabiegalski goes into topics such as complexity, mindfulness, ambidexterity, quantum, indigenous, and other constructs that prove useful for improving both businesses and lives. Eric spends time unpacking *unthinking* and how to tell a story as a way to exercise this interesting concept. One thing that rang true for me was that it's not the knowledge that I have that is important but rather that I am constantly learning. UNTHINK is definitely a book for those who strive to achieve excellence at work and wisdom in life."
—CAPTAIN TODD W. CRAMER
U.S. Navy Virginia Class Nuclear Submarine Commander, Retired

"'Unthinking,' as described in Dr. Zabiegalski's book *Unthink, All You Have To Do Is Nothing*, is the perfect explanation for a technique wise pilots teach: 'Wind your watch.' In any sudden emergency, it is vital to *wind your watch*, that is, pause, take a breath, and focus on something mundane, like twisting a watch dial. This neurological hack frees the active conscious mind to surrender to the sub-conscious. This allows embattled pilots to more easily become aware of other crewmembers (coworkers), sounds, lights, smells, or other physical and emotional stimuli in the environment. Without responding too quickly in a reactive, uncoordinated, or incorrect way, they're able to stop or preclude deadly error chains and win the day. Dr. Z elevates and unpacks this concept and others, expanding their applicability to everyone, not just old-head pilots. Anywhere awareness, effectiveness, and success can be enhanced by letting the whole mind, rather than just the analytical part, engage in the challenges faced, *Unthink* can show you the way. Thoughtful book. Now 'wind your watch,' learn to *unthink*.
—MICHAEL W. EATON
Former Air Force 2 pilot and now captain at a major U.S. airline

"Wow! Brilliant! *Unthink* brings to light how the mind can be pro-ductively balanced for the best you. There's been much research on the mind and thinking, but none I've run across has made the intimate, what Dr. Rosabeth Kanter would describe as the 'zoomed in,' connections that *Unthink* communicates. The icing on the cake all readers will benefit from is how Dr. Zabiegalski masterfully shares how the reader can use storytelling as a way to exercise and master 'unthinking.' Well done!"
—ERIC GAFFORD
Dassault Community of Experts (COE) Data Analysis Chairman
COE Leadership Committee Board Member

"If you're leafing through these pages presuming this is another self-help, how-to book, read on. If you go to work every day having minimally satisfying interactions with others, read UNTHINK and change it. If you're aware how the world affects you and want to do something about it, read on. If you're aware how distractions run your life and want to get a handle on living, take a look at UNTHINK. We walk and talk every day behind a filter of bias and prejudgment inherent and learned. Under this umbrella we're on autopilot, under control without being aware. Try *unthinking* your thoughts, your actions, and yourself. With Dr. Z's small steps, the insights of this book can give you a new way to live."

—MING DIAZ
Retired, U.S. Government, Tucson, AZ

"*Unthink* has challenged me to re-evaluate how I process information, refocusing my conscious mind on the present and improving the performance of my teams. *Unthink* gives me a glimpse of the manager I could become."

—PAUL SCOTT
Critical Incident Inspector, Sussex Police, UK, Retired

"I found Dr. Z's UNTHINK to be a terrific enjoyable read. It tells a story and is not just an instruction manual. UNTHINK is an introduction to the proper use of the mind. It is a 'must read' for anyone changing life direction, whether it's their own decision or forced upon them. A road map guide to finding your own path and becoming a better version of yourself, UNTHINK is a primer for anyone hoping to be a better problem solver and calmer individual."

—BILL NICHOLS
Captain, *William B. Tennison* bugeye log-hull boat (1899), the second-oldest registered passenger vessel in the US and National Historic Landmark

"UNTHINK is exactly as it's prefaced. I found myself outside my normal thought processes, focusing on different aspects and angles of perception on work, personal, and social interaction not previously considered. Surprising! UNTHINK is at a much higher level of reading than the title and premise suggest, challenging me to back up at times. To better understand Eric's concepts and consider their application, I had to *think*, before I could *unthink*. This book is well put together and flows easily for the relaxed, alert, inquisitive mind, a great read for the ready audience. Let Dr. Z teach you to UNTHINK!"

—JAY PERKINS
National Bass Tournament Competitor

"Dr. Zabiegalski has a unique ability to convey timely concepts of tomorrow, today. The theories, complexities, and behaviors that live beyond traditional cultural norms are presented and distilled here for the reader to consider. Eric's book entertains, teaches, and inspires while still leaving room to draw your own conclusions and dream."

—PHILIP WOLF

Founder and CEO of Cultivating Spirits and CashoM
Co-Founder, Hispanola Health Partners

"In today's ever busier world, we <u>need</u> to learn the art and science of *unthink*ing. From research to reflection and questions, from story to practical application, Dr. Zabiegalski equips the reader with rich insights not just for business leaders, but for people of all walks of life to tune out the destructive noise and tune in to the wisdom around us and within us."

—ASHLEY S. FREEMAN, MBA

International bestselling author, *The Path to Your Career Purpose*
Founder & CEO, Flourishing Work LLC

"*Unthink* is an invitation to seek the flow where reasoning and intuition, mind and heart, exploring and exploiting co-exist to complement, empower, and ultimately free each other. This book is not intended to give you the answers; instead, it constantly triggers the questions and curiosities necessary to pursue an ambidextrous life."

—SVEN LAUCH

Director, EyesUp Training

"My first impression of UNTHINK was a take-off on Gloria Steinem I'd heard some time ago. 'The first problem for all of us is not to learn, but to unlearn outer teachings.' It's all inside. Dr. Zabiegalski dives into the diversity within the decision-making process and offers an array of poignant pieces and skillfully crafted soliloquies to take the reader on a journey inside their thinking and expand their thoughtmosphere. That journey is full of insight and inspiration to rise up to a new living awareness in observational capacity and operational congruency in a new world. His expertise and practical application of the leading-edge philosophy and science creates the opportunity for the reader to explore concepts and conundrums in opportunistic fashion. It's a win for all. *UNTHINK* draws on ancient knowledge and modern science, merging them synergistically in an eloquent and thought-provoking experience for the reader. Dr. Zabiegalski expands on the philosophy of *The Rise of the Ambidextrous Organization*, being exploitive and explorative, and applies his skill as a bricoleur to business, life, and relationships with practical examples and inspiring stories that produce an empathic resonance with their sense-making toward creating our future together in business and in life. A true thought-leader for our time, Eric's deep inquiry and understanding shine in this work that, when read, will literally cause an 'upwising' in you."

—ZEN BENEFIEL, DD, MA, MBA, TLC
Executive Director, Live and Let Live Foundation
Host, *One World in a New World*

"*Unthink*: your guide through a changing world. According to Albert Einstein, one of the greatest minds of the 20th century, '*The intuitive mind is a sacred gift and the rational mind is a faithful servant. We have created a society that honors the servant and has forgotten the gift.*' If you've ever wondered how we can rectify this mistake, Dr. Eric Zabiegalski's new book, *Unthink: All You Have To Do Is Nothing*, provides clear signposts along the road to remembering and honoring the sacred gift. It does so by reminding us that we are multidimensional beings, gifted with consciousness, intuition, wisdom, creativity, and compassion, and capable of navigating our way through and beyond our changing reality in multiple ways. This book comes to us at a time when the potentials of AI, robotics, and nano technology (to name a few) are rocking the foundations of our world. Not only are the paradigms of yesterday no longer working, they're obsolete in the age of new technologies. *Unthinking* provides a way forward by putting the multi-dimensional human being back in the driver's seat. Zabiegalski's book shows us how ethical storytelling, which redrafts our stories and reimagines the storyteller, incorporates ancient and modern wisdom in a world gutted with data, information, and knowledge. Ethical storytelling doesn't just emphasize the relevance of the personal in a hier-archical, institutionalized world, it's one of our most important

tools for weaving wisdom, intuition, and consciousness into our rapidly changing world. *Unthink. All You Have To Do Is Nothing* is an important handbook for those willing to engage with simple yet effective strategies for facing our uncertain and sometimes frightening future."
—DR. CARMEL FINNAN
Communication Consultant and Writer

"In his newest written adventure, Dr. Zabiegalski lets you dive deeper into his ideas by following his train of thought from examining paradigms and ways of knowing, our organizations as ambidextrous organizations, our workplace as an environment of diversity, the importance of storytelling in our social and organizational lives, and various disruptive factors we face, to our own personal dilemmas that often reflect fears and doubts, but also hopes and aspirations. If you have ever wondered about many of the things around you, if you have questioned some assumptions that other people take for granted, if you want to learn and dig deeper, then this book is for you, regardless of who and what you are—a CEO, a low-level manager, an employee, or an ordinary person who wants to make sense of the world. While you may not find all the answers here, Eric will make you think critically, abandon your assumptions, and dive into the sea of the unknown that is uncertain but waiting to become and emerge through your own observing, thinking, or just being. Eventually, Eric leads you to a state where you simply observe, feel, and enter into the state of nonthinking and deep presence and awareness where you can finally meet yourself, gain confidence in something greater than yourself, go into the flow of life, and finally see the situations and people around you in truer colors. Make it a habit to question everything, to think critically, to learn and experience, and to learn to be still and not think. Let Eric help you enjoy your ride!"
—PROFESSOR NATAŠA RUPČIĆ, PHD
Department for Organization and Management
Faculty of Economics and Business
University of Rijeka, Croatia

"An excellent inspiring book by Dr. Eric Zabiegalski. Like no other, Eric thinks across different fields, from storytelling to quantum physics, connecting them to organizations and everyday life. I recommend Eric as a keynote speaker and inspiration on any occasion and echo Dr Z's challenge to learn to UNTHINK."
—JENS LARSEN
Co-founder of True Storytelling Institute
Co-author of *True Storytelling—Seven Principles for an Ethical and Sustainable Change-Management Strategy*
Copenhagen, Denmark
"True Storytelling sets people free."

Table of Contents

Foreword

"The primary function of the mind is to discern," someone once said to me, and it triggered a question—"Where does the information the mind is discerning come from?"

Looking back at my life, I identified two ways people discern information. You either rely on the world around you as the source and discern only between opinions and knowledge, or your mind discerns between two sources of information, external and internal, the world and the heart. The latter is transformational. It certainly transformed my life. However, accessing information from the heart requires what Eric calls unthinking.

The impact of unthinking on my life has been profound. Growing up in communist East Germany, the regime systematically indoctrinated me. I believed in it and was about to fulfill my life's dream aligned with the values of the system. Then one day, November 11, 1989, the fall of the Berlin Wall pulled the carpet on which I firmly stood from under my feet.

Ten years later, I faced the fact that during the first 15 years of my life, I only learned to discern between filtered opinions and pre-interpreted information from around me. For a further 10 years, I tried to find a new happy place in a world using thinking as a way of discerning. It didn't work. What was going wrong?

These days, our mind gets overloaded with external unfiltered information that is relentlessly funneled into the brain. The mind's way of discerning between right and wrong or good and bad no longer works well and leads to increasing defensiveness and divisiveness. To make sense of the chaos, we create more and more labels to group anything and everything until the sheer number of labels leads to more information overload. Healthily positioning ourselves has become an impossible task.

What revolutionized my life is the unthinking way of discerning, the way of connectedness and relatedness. It positions the mind in its rightful place between my heart (internal information) and the world around me (external information). In that position, the mind does not have to decide between right and wrong, good or bad. Instead, it now discerns where and how to connect and relate my internal information—my values—to the external world.

The more I practiced it over the last 20 years, the more I began to relate to the world around me instead of trying to position myself in it. Over time, I became less concerned about what to do when, where, and how and more driven by learning who I am and how I can connect, relate, and contribute to that complex world around me.

Reading Eric's *Unthink* made my heart jump for joy. He compiled stories and research and invites you to start your own journey to reconnect your mind to your heart—your thinking and your unthinking. Many of his suggestions I have practiced and perfected on my journey to recover from a mind of indoctrination.

Read *Unthink* as an invitation to seek the flow where reasoning and intuition, mind and heart, exploring and exploiting co-exist to complement, empower, and ultimately free each other. Allow Eric's book to trigger the questions and curiosity necessary to pursue an ambidextrous life in a chaotic world—personally and professionally. And if you experience unpleasant emotions while reading, then remember a little piece of wisdom from me: Your unpleasant emotions are triggered by your set of values, not by what is written or said. They are signposts to your values, identity, and purpose and want to connect you to your deepest authenticity—your heart. Let your emotions help you unthink.

—SVEN LAUCH
Emotional Intelligence Coach
Trainer and Speaker
Founder and Director of Eyes Up

Preface

Though I'm a native Washing-
tonian, born in the District of Columbia, I
spent my formative years in San Diego,
California. The San Diego of the 1970s
was a magical place to be a kid. French
naval officer, oceanographer, and
filmmaker Jacques Cousteau kept his
submarine docked in Mission Bay,
Theodor Geisel (Dr. Seuss) lived just over
the next hill in La Jolla and we were
invited to his house annually for parties,
and SeaWorld San Diego had the original
"Shamu," the killer whale, performing
along with a one-third-scale pirate ship crewed by (real)
chimpanzees dressed as pirates! Most of my free time in those days
was devoted to skateboards and bicycles. I walked around barefoot,
was always energized and engaged, and didn't have to think too
much. Everything made intuitive sense, and I knew what I wanted
to do next—until the day the well-dressed, polite, and caring people
came to my door.

I was a latch-key kid in those days, as both of my parents
worked, and after school I would get my homework done and was
free to watch television until dinnertime. One day when I was 12,
there was a knock on the door, and I opened it to find two young
people wearing white shirts and ties and carrying pamphlets asking
to speak to my mother or father. I told them they weren't home yet,
and they asked if they could drop off some reading material and
speak to me for a moment before they left. I obliged. I forgot what
church they said they represented, but they informed me they were
on a dire mission to warn the good citizens of the city to move out
of the country before it was too late. Now was the time to move
families and businesses to Canada, as America was soon to be

punished for its sins and crimes against humanity. The United States, they said, was about to become a "smoking hole" and everyone in it would perish. "You seem like a nice kid," they said. "Save yourself and don't forget to tell your parents we came by. Have a nice day." I suddenly had a lot to think about.

When my mother returned home a half-hour later, I was beside myself. I quickly sat her down on the couch and nervously recounted the dark situation we were in and what the sincere people at the door said we needed to do to save our family. In a moment, it felt as if I had suddenly gone from a carefree child in an inspirational world that made sense to one that was fearful, dark, and confusing. When I was finally done laying out the timeline and the logistics of our evacuation plan, she told me not to worry and that these things were not likely to happen. She said that what those people said, though convincing, was just their opinion and not fact. She then related a story. "When I was a little girl growing up in the early 1940s, there were a lot of people saying the same kinds of things: the world was going to end. It was a difficult and scary time for many people, and many people were fearful and full of illogical opinions." My mother's caring advice and story on that day made all the difference and offered a valuable perspective I will always remember.

What happened back then feels a lot like what's happening today—perhaps only on a much larger scale due to global communications and social media. Humanity is in a period of rapid growth and radical change. Many people are fearful and have been conditioned to be so by seemingly caring and convincing people, including people of authority. But many of these people are irresponsible, ignorant, or have an agenda, peddling an emotionally driven and irrational religion with their starched white shirts and glossy pamphlets. What they promoted flies in the face of intuition, ethics, and rationality but otherwise looks and sounds convincing. What can we do? I hope you will find the answers in this book.

One of the early reviewers of UNTHINK asked me why I wrote it, and I didn't have an immediate answer. "What was my intent?" they said. I summarily tried to dismiss the question, being caught up in the whirlwind of last-minute details in getting the book to the editor. These will likely be the last words I write in this book. But the thought stayed with me; it wouldn't go away. It didn't help that knowing something of that person, their reverence and seriousness for thought, I knew their inquiry was sincere. Also, how often do people ask such genuine questions of one another nowadays? It's rare. I couldn't ignore it. Besides that, I'd always heard that Europeans don't make "small talk" like Americans do. If they ask you something, it's because they want to know, so here's my attempt at an answer.

As the researcher Karl Weick said on the process of sense-making, "*How do I know what I think until I see what I've said?*" I'm not a hundred percent certain what my intent was for writing *UNTHINK*, but hearing the words come out of my own head helps. I think my intent in writing this book has something to do with the exhilaration and joy of that childlike wonder I experienced growing up. And, occasionally catching glimpses of it now as an adult speeding by me outside my railway car window, I had a yearning to get back to that feeling and place. Think about it: What if we as adults could see that scenery with those same young eyes every day? I came to realize that the pursuit of wanting that feeling back has been an unspoken lifetime "sub-occupation," with hit or miss results and no discernible algorithms to repeat and share with the world, perhaps until now. Sometimes wrenching it (contentment and joy) from the hands of the universe, sometimes accidentally stumbling onto it, sometimes having it lovingly gifted, and some-times orchestrating it, I still couldn't seem to organically make it happen, or happen consistently. There must be a way. And, as my adolescence taught me too often, bartering my health for it, a few moments facsimile of that earlier "authentic" joy at the expense of my future self, wasn't sustainable or smart. Eventually a reckoning comes due upon your future self, and most likely with it a bill too high to pay. Manufacturing artificial feelings was harmful, unsus-tainable, and expensive. In the hauntingly beautiful words and melody of American singer-songwriter Matt Nathanson in the song *All We Are* (2007): "*I kept falling over, I kept looking backward, I went broke believing that the simple should be hard.*" That was me. The idea here is that "life" should not always be so tortuously hard as it too often is, and if it is, you're probably doing something wrong and could be doing it better, so why not fix it. Also, there's a *thought-intent* here about *kindness*, not to others but instead this time to you.

We've commonly heard throughout our lives to be kind to one another, and this is a virtuous imperative. But less common is the message to *be kind to yourself.* You are a good person doing the best you can with the tools you have learned. If it doesn't *feel* right, it's likely not right, so *learn, unlearn,* and *relearn* what you need to, do whatever you have to do, and change things.

Get out of, and away from, your conscious head and silence and subjugate the crow of criticism (your inner voice) that is always talking to you. Relegating it to the proper place among the rank and file of useful tools in your head where it can help instead of hurt you is part of the intent of UNTHINK. My intent also had to do with clearing away all of the baggage and layers of sediment we accumulate throughout our lives as we grow and age. In UNTHINK, I use the metaphor of each of us as a river beginning as a stream. We originate from a crystal-clear spring and end as a wide overgrown, muddy delta, full of dirt, silt, reeds, marshland vegetation, and all manner of creatures, both benevolent and menacing. The abstractions we accumulate throughout life contribute to this end state landscape. It's a beautiful, complex, and rich one, but it's also complicated. How can we understand it and find our original selves hiding within? This end picture we become as adults should not necessarily be taken for the things that are real, honest, and *us*, particularly if they're harmful or we do not want them.

As you may discern from the early reviewers' comments in the front of UNTHINK, this book is not so much a *how-to* as it is a self-help book and resource manual. My hope is that you think of it as such. Pick it up, put it down, write in the margins, argue and have conversations with it and with others, and get what you need from it. The only thing we have control of in life is ourselves—our thoughts, actions, and how we react in a constantly moving and spinning world around us. My intent for writing this book and my intent for you is that, read it or don't read it, you learn to *unthink* and enjoy the ride of this wonderful life with the living world and your fellow human beings.

Fast forward 50 years from that 10-year-old boy full of wonderment growing up in Southern California. When Sven Lauch agreed to write the foreword to this book, I became very excited, though I didn't entirely know why. I knew something of Sven's work and the lives he touched and transformed with his insights and advice, but there was something more, something connected to the message in this book. If you look closely at the early reviewers in the front of UNTHINK, you may notice a curious algorithm: It's fairly asymmetric. Other than the mental acumen required in each of their professions and perhaps a common message to leave the well-beaten path in the name of curiosity, or necessity, the reviewers don't follow any other patterns in relation to one another. I also readily admit that in addition to the serious thinkers I knew and admired from different walks of life which I asked to provide reviews, I also reached out in the blind to some big influencers of humanity and literary inspirations shining in the night sky whom I didn't know well or even at all. I rolled the dice and took a chance. Sven was one of those luminaries I reached out to, and while he wasn't the farthest light I reached for (we'd spoken before), because I knew his story, I knew he was one of the brightest ones.

Teenage years are fragile for any adolescent, regardless of your nationality or predicament. But if you're a 15-year-old boy growing up in communist East Germany in 1989, your world shatters like a piece of safety glass when your parents sit you down and tell you everything you ever knew just disappeared overnight. Believe it or not, for Sven, prior to the falling of the Berlin Wall and the dissolution of communism, life felt good. Food and housing were cheap, and day-to-day life was comfortable, predictable, structured, and choreographed. The walls around him, as far as Sven was concerned, were erected to keep you and I out, not to keep him in. On that day in November, everything in the world changed. For Sven and his family, there was no joy that day, no sadness, just shock. In his words, his dreams died that day along with his worldview and his purpose. Sven had to feel his way out of the shapeless dark from a once structured, predictable, mapped-out life that had been laid out for him from birth to death. It was a life where he didn't have to think (different from unthinking) and neither did his family, who were just as lost and unable to console him. Contrary to popular belief, captivity can be freeing and comfortable when you're institutionalized. Prisoners are told when and what to eat, when to sleep and wake, and when to recreate and work. Rather than freedom of choice, they have freedom *from* choice. Set adrift, Sven had to suddenly unlearn everything he knew, and then learn to ask questions and form opinions, create his own structure and a new worldview, and find his own meaning and purpose. It took him 30 years to do and a lot of soul searching, depression, revelation, determination, humility, and grit. What did Sven learn in the end and what does he know now? He learned that the walls he had grown up with around him were *never* around him but were *in* him, and that the future has no limits, just edges of distinction. And he now knows to walk to those edges and peer over the side, considering what's there without prejudgment or knee-jerk reaction.

After I asked Sven if he would write the foreword and read what he wrote I realized what it was, why I had gotten so excited. Perhaps I intuitively knew it all along without consciously knowing. Sven had taught himself the art of *unthinking* on his journey long before I wrote about it. To unlearn and relearn, use intuition and intellect, develop a *proprioception of thought*, and question everything. Now he helps others to do the same—to *unthink*.

Introduction

Get out of your head and get into the world. It needs you. There are some very interesting things happening in the world today—curious things, exciting things, and menacing things. It's a great time to be alive, so get into the fray and live. If you jump in with an open heart, an open mind, and a commitment to be of help, you will be successful in any endeavor. How can you do it? The answer is simply "unthink." When you get out of your head, your myopic vision refocuses and you see farther and with more clarity, with the sight of a falcon.

In a recent conversation, a neighbor described 12 years of sobriety from alcohol. They said something surprising: One of the secrets of breaking the dual grip of addiction (physical and mental) was to let your troubling thoughts go to a higher power. They said it didn't matter who, or what—God, the universe, whatever. This was the secret of those who achieved lasting success.

This point takes on new relevance and intrigue when we add what we have learned of "thought" being a physical, reflexive muscle movement. As such, is there truly any mysterious and elusive "mental" aspect to addiction, or is it all physical in varying degrees? Is it possible we have simply overlooked this subtle aspect of the reflexive muscle movement of mental addiction and that now knowing this would make all the difference?

According to physicist David Bohm, the mental side of habit or addiction is infinitely harder than the physical, as our thoughts are quick to remind us of things we have done before and of things that we like (e.g., those that create endorphins) or find comforting, secure, or exhilarating. It's a dangerous and frustrating treadmill of the observer and the observed when we are simultaneously the problem and the solution.

This goes back to our discussions of the "I" and the "me" that make up the self. It splits us into a subject/object dilemma in which we are at once powerful and powerless, and it is left to us to decide which and when. Most of us are unaware of this war going on inside. Sure, we're aware of conflict, stress, and anxiety but are unaware of what it is or what to do to reconcile it. So at times we let ourselves be objectified as a nonhuman "thing" or characterize ourselves as "poor me" and "little old me."

Can you imagine your life if you could easily determine the origins of your thoughts and then decide on their validity? If you could discriminate between an intuition and a memory, between a bias and an observation, reflection, or awareness? Could you imagine a world in which everyone had similar superpowers and confidently and calmly executed behavior on a true picture of now, without assuming, without judging, without confusing? Such a world *is* possible, but it starts with each of us making the effort to quiet the reflexive thoughts in our heads and suspend them until we check in with awareness and observation and question what thought is telling us against what we see and sense.

Some people's minds are noisy places, and their thoughts never stop telling them things. That's okay. You can be a Chatty Kathy in your head but know how and when to quiet that voice and don't verbalize everything unless the time and circumstances are right.

When I was a flight engineer aircrew member in the Air Force, I sat behind and in the middle of two other crew members, the pilot, and the copilot. As long as everything was normal and you weren't talking on the radio, you could ramble on endlessly about pretty much anything you wanted. The exception was when the plane got below 10,000 feet, which the pilot called a "sterile cockpit." That meant stop talking. We were in a critical phase of flight, and activities were going to get time compressed. As if by conditioning, when we entered this phase of flight, not only did my mouth turn off, but so did my brain. In this compression of time and space, I experienced singular and linear thoughts directly linked to the flight checklist on my lap and the moment of my surroundings. Similar to what an athlete calls being "in the zone" or what Mihaly Csikszentmihalyi described as the state of "flow, "a focused mental state conducive to productivity in which one often loses track of time. I was executing proprioception of thought, the proper order and processing of awareness, observation, and thought. Without this training and ability to recondition the mind at will, Captain Chesley "Sully" Sullenberger wouldn't have been able to turn the Hudson River into a landing strip, saving 155 lives. American football player Gale Sayers would not have been the most difficult player to tackle in football history. My advice for you? Develop this skill of "flow," learn to enter the "zone," get out of your head, look around, and unthink!

In my last book, I talked about finding balance through models, mostly in business, and the often unfortunate predicament of human life. In this book, I address balance again but in a much more important area, the human mind, and in a much more important place, you. It's my opinion that the best books take you on a journey, delivering you to a new destination, and you are changed at the end. That is also the promise of this book.

The Promise of Unthinking

The deeper I descend into the rabbit hole in my thinking and learning of human cognition, the more I discover about this hall of mirrors that is the human mind. The promise of *Unthink* is to make the reader aware of the differences between the conscious and subconscious mind and when each is, and should be, at the helm of our thinking, driving our life. There are researchers who say we spend as much as 90% of our waking day drawing from the subconscious, and while you might immediately think this is the perfect recipe for *unthinking*, it's actually a terrible state of affairs. Do you remember the first or last Raiders of the Lost Ark movies in which the sacred Ark of the Covenant is stored in a vast Army Depot warehouse? (in Tobyhanna, PA, incidentally)? Well, your subconscious mind is kind of like that warehouse, a cavernous storage space. And oh, by the way, there's no one in there. You have to go in and rummage around for stored information yourself. This suggests a couple of interesting things. First, when your conscious mind goes back there opening file cabinets, looking into shelves, and walking down long hallways, it's distracted and not paying attention to the *here and now*, what's happening in the present. This could render you anywhere from aloof, to dumb, to dead if you think of it like driving your car down the road while at the same time looking and reaching into the back seat to retrieve something from a box. The second thing that comes to mind is the idea that the knowledge in your subconscious storehouse might be good stuff—a lot of it is—but it might also be stale, old, and outdated. It may be inappropriate or irrelevant, not serve you anymore, or just be flat out wrong. That bad thing that happened to you when you were 5 probably won't happen again if you're 55. So if you were initially thinking that *unthinking* would be an instruction book for how to turn off the conscious rational mind and let something else take over (the subconscious, maybe?), you would be wrong. Like I said, there's no one back there. You can't really turn off the conscious mind anyway; if you tried, it would just run into your subconscious warehouse and stay there 24/7, disappear, and eventually get lost back there—a terrible situation. Rather, the promise of unthinking is more akin to retraining your conscious mind to do a better job at what it should be doing: management and consultation for you, and additionally teaching you to do a better job training your brain to get the most out of it.

Recently, in the course of two separate conversations in as many days, a newfound friend, Mac Bogert, who wrote a book called *Learning Chaos*, asked me a question in a podcast we were doing: "Why do we lose our childlike wonder?" "Oh! I think I know this one," I thought. At some point in our childhood we're told to *stop asking so many questions*, and we grow fearful of questions. There's still a part of us that wants to have experience, but these end up being curated experiences, really grounded in things we've done before—safe bets, the familiar and known about, or the heavily researched. Incidentally, remember that giant subconscious warehouse in the mind I talked about? Mac says if we take in information, learning, see, hear, read, think, or sense something and we can't remember it, it's not a storage problem but probably a recall problem. Why is that? Mac says that the brain can store 280 quintillion (280,000,000,000,000,000,000) bits of memory. That's the equivalent of 35 billion gigabytes of hard drive space, virtually limitless. So why do we remember some things for our entire lives and have an easy time recalling certain information and not others?

I don't know the answer to that, but I do know that I remember the slogan on the label of Budweiser beer, 46 words, and I have no idea why I know that. I haven't recalled it in over 40 years, but I could recite it cold from memory right now. While I don't know how to turn on/turn off those super memory abilities, there are things we can do to improve our memories using tricks learned by the ancient Greeks leveraging the brain's natural evolutionary abilities. We will talk about those later.

The other conversation was one I listened to between one of my heroes, Dr. Iain McGilchrist, and Alex Ramirez, in which they discussed the origins of the word *experience*.

Definitions and Terms

Before we dive into unthinking, let's cover a few important definitions and concepts.

Unthinking. The idea of using the vast storehouse of the intuitive, gut feeling, subconscious mind and physical body, as opposed to ignoring, blocking, distrusting, overtalking, or shouting it down with the conscious mind. Unthinking is a combination and triangulation of other senses and sensations like *awareness* and *observation*, combined with rational *thought*, and involves the mutual contribution of both the conscious and subconscious mind together.

Exploitation. The use and refinement of existing knowledge within an organization's internal domains, associated with existing improvements, increased efficiency, and incremental adjustments.

Exploration. The search for and pursuit of new knowledge within an organization's external domains, accompanied by variety generation, distant search, risk-taking, experimentation, and discovery.

Organizational culture. A pattern of shared basic assumptions, artifacts, values, and symbols learned by a group as it solves its problems of external adaptation and internal integration that has worked well enough to be considered valid and taught to new members as the correct way to perceive, think, and feel.

Organizational learning. Different from a *learning organization*, it is a structured and administrative process for detecting and correcting errors and is an overarching umbrella encompassing any type of structured learning or teaching required by an organization.

Learning organization. An organization skilled at dynamically creating, acquiring, and transferring knowledge and modifying behavior to reflect new knowledge and insights in real time. It includes all potential types of learning that could emerge, including intentional, unintentional, structured, nonstructured, formal, and informal.

Organizational ambidexterity. The ability of an organization to both explore and exploit—to compete in mature technologies and markets where efficiency, control, and incremental improvement are prized and to also compete in new technologies and markets where flexibility, autonomy, and experimentation are needed.

Worldview. A collection of attitudes, values, stories, and expectations about the world around us which inform our thoughts and actions.

Field theory. A psychological theory that examines patterns of interaction between individuals and the total field of their environment.

Indigenous ways of knowing. An epistemology that is a type of Indigenous wisdom relying on many forms of intelligence, including interpersonal, kinesthetic, and spiritual intelligence, and involving natural models, nonlinear thinking, and quantum thinking.

Western ways of knowing. An epistemology that is a type of Western thinking and wisdom relying on decontextualized compartmentalized knowledge broken into disciplines, like capitalism, industrialism, technology, mechanized, linear, and Newtonian models (and of late quantum models) to explain physics, the natural world, and the universe and having pragmatic (practical) views and values.

Storytelling. The social and cultural activity of sharing stories and narratives for entertainment, education, cultural preservation, or the instillation of moral values, often with improvisation, theatrics, or embellishment. Different from other communication or information dissemination methods, storytelling can utilize and employ all the senses and engages both the right and left hemispheres of the brain in its transmission and reception. Crucial elements of stories and storytelling include *plot, characters,* and *narrative point of view.*

Sensemaking. The process by which people give meaning to collective experience. The ongoing retrospective development of plausible images that rationalize what people do. Introduced by Karl E. Weick in the 1970s, it was an attempt to shift organizational theorists toward a focus on the *processes that constitute the meaning of decisions* that are enacted in behavior and away from a traditional focus on decision-making. Weick famously said in his book *Sensemaking in Organizations* (1995), "How do I know what I think until I see what I've said?"

Arrogance of ignorance. Coined by me, the idea of knowing that you don't know something (piece of data or information) of relative or contextual importance and not caring about your ignorance or caring to know. A phrase of negative connotation, it's an intentional bull- or pig-headedness borne of personal intent or agenda which is (initially) hidden or unknown.

Multiverse theory. A theory that proposes a hypothetical group of multiple universes called "parallel universes" or "alternate universes," which together comprise everything that exists to include the entirety of space, time, matter, energy, information, and the physical laws and constants that describe them. I suggest in this book a different spin on this theory centered around the idea that "we," humanity, is each a universe unto ourselves, separate and connected to others, as we are made of the building block elements of the universe.

Theory of everything (TOE). Also called final theory, ultimate theory, unified field theory, or master theory, a hypothetical, singular, all-encompassing, coherent theoretical framework of physics that fully explains and links all the aspects of the universe. One of the major unsolved problems in physics, String theory and M-theory have been proposed as TOEs. Two theoretical frameworks have been developed that, together, most closely (for now) resemble a TOE, theories upon which all modern physics rests: general relativity (focusing on large-scale bodies and high mass, planets, stars, galaxies, etc.) and quantum mechanics (focusing on three nongravitational forces—strong nuclear, weak nuclear, and electromagnetic). General relativity and quantum mechanics have been separately validated scientifically, but a theory connecting the two has yet to be proven, i.e., a theory of everything. In this book I propose a theory connecting the two.

Proprioception of thought. An idea suggested by late physicist David Bohm that incorporates cognitively triangulating *awareness*, *observation*, and *thought* to increase and better utilize perception and intelligence and to improve the experiencing of physical and mental reality employing both the conscious and unconscious intuitive (unthinking) mind. The term *proprioception* is borrowed from physical therapy and involves the orchestration and subtle movement of the muscles and skeleton.

Fantasy. Different from creativity or imagination, a specu- lative fiction involving magical elements typically set in a fictional universe, sometimes inspired by mythology and folklore but otherwise not tethered to reality, nature, natural laws, logic, or any plausible type of coherent foundation as a basis. It is whimsy or fancy. Fantasy is distinguished from science and facts, creativity and imagination by often using magic, magic practitioners, crea- tures or other created supernatural elements. No logic or logical scientific or technological extrapolation is necessary.

Creativity. Derived from a Latin word meaning to create or make, it includes convergent and divergent thinking and concep- tual blending. Different from fantasy or imagination, it is a phenomenon whereby something new and valuable is formed by the mind. The created item may be intangible (such as an idea, a scientific theory, a musical composition, or a joke) or a physical object (such as an invention, a printed literary work, or painting). Creativity and intelligence are thought of as overlapping constructs; creativity is a subset of intelligence, and intelligence is a subset of creativity. Creativity is found in psychology, business, social science, cognitive science, engineering, technology, mathematics, and other disciplines mixing the relationships between intelligence and creativity.

Imagination. Linked with cognition and a cognitive process used in mental functioning, of which visual imagery is a type, it is different from fantasy or creativity and is the production or simulation of novel objects, sensations, and ideas in the mind without any immediate input of the senses. It's the forming of experiences in one's mind, which can be re-creations or "imaging" of past experiences, such as memories with imagined changes, or completely invented and possibly fantastic scenes. Imagination differs from fantasy in that it is an "imaging" and imagining of something formerly known but with changes or variations. Imagination helps make knowledge applicable in solving problems and is fundamental to integrating experience and learning. As an approach to building theory, it is called "disciplined imagination." Imaginative thought may be associated with rational thought on the assumption that both activities can involve cognitive processes that may underpin thinking about possibilities.

Unthinking Models

Are there models for unthinking? Currently the answer is no, but perhaps if there were drafts of such models that could inform future better "unthinking" models, they would look like one of these. Personally, I love models, but I don't fall in love with them; I keep them in perspective and at bay. I understand their purpose and the limits of their usefulness. Not everyone does, however. Some become so in love with the models they've created for understanding and navigating the world that they ignore reality and its embodied context. The left hemisphere of our brain loves them too. Think of these models as helping you find your ultimate unthinking model.

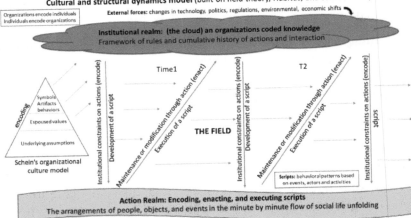

Cultural and structural dynamics model (built on field theory, Habitus, and Structuration)

Organizations encode individuals
Individuals encode organizations

External forces: changes in technology, politics, regulations, environmental, economic shifts

Institutional realm: (the cloud) an organizations coded knowledge
Framework of rules and cumulative history of actions and interaction

Time1

T2

Symbols
Artifacts
behaviors

Espoused values

Underlying assumptions

Schein's organizational
culture model

encoding

Institutional constraints on actions (encode)

Development of a script

Maintenance or modification through action (enact)

Execution of a script

THE FIELD

Institutional constraints on actions (encode)

Development of a script

Maintenance or modification through action (enact)

Execution of a script

Institutional constraints on actions (encode)

script

Scripts: behavioral patterns based
on events, actors and activities

Action Realm: Encoding, enacting, and executing scripts
The arrangements of people, objects, and events in the minute by minute flow of social life unfolding

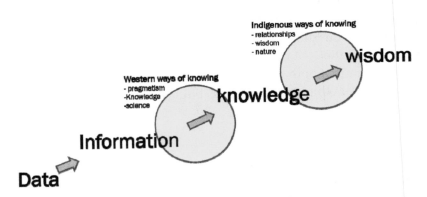

Indigenous ways of knowing
- relationships
- wisdom
- nature

wisdom

Western ways of knowing
- pragmatism
- Knowledge
- science

knowledge

Information

Data

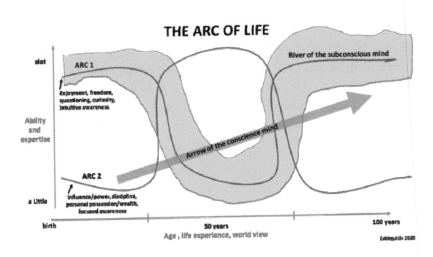

THE ARC OF LIFE

alot

ARC 1

River of the subconscious mind

Enjoyment, freedom,
questioning, curiosity,
intuitive awareness

Ability
and
expertise

Arrow of the conscience mind

ARC 2

Influence/power, discipline,
personal possession/wealth,
focused awareness

a Little

birth

50 years

100 years

Age , life experience, world view

Lakingalahi 2020

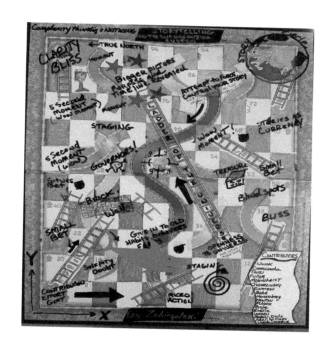

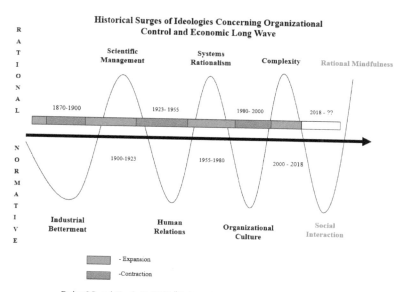

Historical Surges of Ideologies Concerning Organizational Control and Economic Long Wave

R
A
T
I
O
N
A
L

Scientific Management

Systems Rationalism

Complexity

Rational Mindfulness

1870-1900

1923- 1955

1980- 2000

2018 - ??

N
O
R
M
A
T
I
V
E

1900-1923

1955-1980

2000 - 2018

Industrial Betterment

Human Relations

Organizational Culture

Social Interaction

- Expansion

-Contraction

Barley, S.R. and Kunda, G. (1992) "Design and devotion: Surges of rational and normative ideologies of control in managerial discourse. ASQ 37(3) Modified by Professor David Schwandt for GW University (2010), updated/modified by E. Zabiegalski for Webster University HR Training and Development, and Management course (2018)

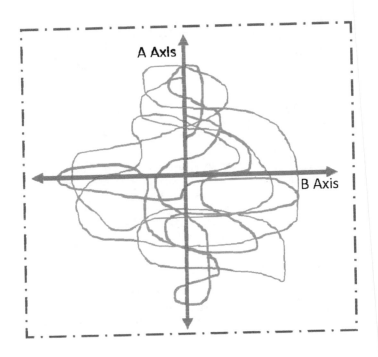

About This Book

To help you get the most from this book, *Unthink* has been designed to tell you stories, paint pictures, take you on a journey, and stretch your current knowledge and thinking on a number of subjects and areas. By the end of it, you will be changed, and there will be no going back.

This book is divided into five parts. The first three parts discuss adopting an unthinking mindset: in business, in everyday life, and in relation to others and the world around you. Afterwards, the last two parts focus on how to begin to unthink, creating the unthinking you and moving forward. The book closes with some final advice on moving through the world and thinking about it.

So if you want to get the most from this book, start by not thinking too hard about getting anything from this book. Just enjoy the read and let your brain take care of the learning and make connections. It will surprise you when something you forgot you read here comes forward later. Your brain, in particular the subconscious mind, will do the heavy lifting; it will take care of the rest. You'll be taking an "unthinking" approach to reading this. Consider it your first exercise. Pick it up when you feel like it, throw it down when you don't, invent thought experiments from it and try them out, reflect, and try new things. Incidentally, my friend Mac also says every time you try something new, like let's say eating with your nondominant hand, you create new brain cells (glial cells) as you make new demands on the brain. Any new chaos encountered increases mental connectivity. That's pretty cool.

The best way I can describe how to successfully unthink is to use an expression from decades past: to first "tune out, and then start tuning in." There are things that we have been conditioned to pay attention to which are turning out to not be that important in life, and others that we have been encouraged to ignore which are turning out to be very important in life. It's the latter that we should pay attention to. What are these things? You will pick up on what those are as you go through this book. It's at once perhaps the most exciting time in human history and the most confusing tumultuous time. It's certainly a time of great transition and upheaval and per- haps that's the significant takeaway—that this is a time of white- water rapids change, and when we get shot out of the strong current of the venturi, we will be in a better place because of it—a new place, and one that is not so frightening and anxious. This book and the journey it takes you on leaves off where my last book, *The Rise of the Ambidextrous Organization*, left you, as an integral part of the employment working machine, and then it transcends it.

PART 1:
UNTHINKING BUSINESS

Crossroads of Cognition: Managing Paradigms and Ways of Knowing

What would you think if I told you to "unthink"? You'd probably look at me funny, tilting your head like an Irish Setter perhaps, trying to understand, and then wouldn't know what to do with such a strange suggestion. It might even cause you to do the opposite—to think more—but unthink is precisely what I'm going to ask you to do.

What do I mean when I say unthink? I mean that we are most *right* when we are in motion, cognitive motion, when we are in a state of learning, questioning, and open-minded thought. We know vastly more in this state of curiosity and questioning and actively engaging our minds than when we park on a thought or a data point and ruminate, covet, or defend it, and when we suspend judgment too. So unthinking is a bit of an intentional misnomer. I'm not suggesting you shut everything down and let your mind wander anywhere and everywhere it wants; rather, that you train it to seek and find greater balance, and, for most of us, that requires suppressing currently overactive and vocal parts of our brains while encouraging and allowing other parts to have a voice. The brain doesn't like to and can't sit idle. It's not good for it to try, either. It needs to have a focused task as opposed to an empty space without purpose. It needs to be employed, exercised, and active.

Do you actively *think* or merely rearrange your prejudices, biases, and judgments? Most of us do the latter, and because organizations are made of people, our companies do this too. My research of the past 7 years has focused on something called organizational ambidexterity, which was the focus of my first book. Introduced in the 1970s, the term *organizational ambidexterity* is defined as the ability of organizations to successfully *exploit* and *explore* their environment for profit and market share. That is

16

difficult for organizations to do, and also for individuals. The point here is that we are creatures of habit, especially if that habit comes with a payout, and even if it might not be so great for us long term or might even be horrible for us. "So what? It feels good, I like it, I'm doing it" is often our feeling. What's the connection between organizational ambidexterity and unthinking? You might think of it in this way. Ambidextrous organizations are companies that have learned to "unthink" collectively. So in this section on business and unthinking, when we're talking about ambidexterity, make that concept synonymous with *unthinking* only on a larger collective scale. It's the idea of finding balance in our thinking, planning, and acting, and between our rational and intuitive minds where and when it applies to the work we do as we explore what unthinking is and what it will ultimately mean to you.

Ambidextrous organizations don't needlessly cling to old paradigms simply because they used them yesterday or because someone says, "That's the way we do things around here." They search for new paradigms to adopt; they create them themselves; and they continually evaluate and challenge the ones they have.

What does it mean to be ambidextrous in an organization, and what does it take? It takes attention to detail, awareness, strength, focus, and effort, and it also takes an intuitive awareness of a bigger picture, relaxation, and a detachment from details—a large- and small-picture view. It sounds more difficult than it is. The brain is a muscle just like every other muscle in the body, susceptible to reflexes and repetition and capable of being conditioned and exercised.

Becoming Ambidextrous

An ambidextrous organization has to be a "learning organization." This is not to be confused with organizational learning. Furthermore, the organization must have a special kind of culture, a special kind of structure, and a special kind of leadership, all built on a different kind of foundation. It's not for the faint of heart. This approach takes courage and emotionally intelligent left- and right-brained thinkers. But while experiencing ambidexterity is not difficult, achieving the highest levels of it *is*, and sustaining it is even harder.

When a paradigm shifts, it requires everyone and everything in the old paradigm to go back to zero, it can have a profound effect on people as well as organizations. In the case of companies like Kodak, Xerox, and Blockbuster, the effect was profoundly bad. Kodak engineers held early patents for a digital camera which were ignored by management and leadership and eventually sold to a Japanese company. Xerox had all but created the infrastructure for an early home computer, with a mouse and computer features we are familiar with today, but was so preoccupied with copiers that it allowed its engineers, inventions, and knowledge capital to be purchased and spirited away by Steve Jobs. Most of us know what happened to Blockbuster at the hands of Netflix after it failed to pay attention to an early buy offer from Netflix, which amounted to what was a paltry sum comparatively, and adapt to a changing market.

But that is not to say that everyone is affected badly when a paradigm shifts. People and organizations that have learned to keep an open mind, that have the foresight and courage to walk out to the edge of an existing paradigm and peer over the edge, can catch a glimpse of what is coming next and can prepare themselves for the changes of the next big thing—or even help co-create it.

Organizational Paradigms

What are paradigms? Think of them as roadmaps or navigational compass headings. Akin to schema, they are familiar and vetted patterns, mental models, frameworks, and shortcuts we create to save time, work more efficiently, and exploit what we already know—and, yes, paradigms contain prejudices, bias, and judgments. That being said, as long as we are walking within the realm of the familiar and using them with thoughtful intent, they're benevolent, helpful, and work great. If organizations and people venture beyond them into new territory or use them carelessly, however, they will find themselves lost and without a useable strategy.

When I started my research on organizational ambidexterity, companies that could both explore and exploit their environments for profit, my expectation was that finding ambidexterity in a company would be like finding a unicorn, but I was wrong. To my surprise, I found that all companies start out ambidextrous but then quickly change. Few organizations were able to sustain ambidextrous behavior; that was the real unicorn. Over 40 years of research on the subject of organizational ambidexterity backed up the notion that *"exploitation drives out exploration."* What does that mean? it's simple. As organizations learn to do something well in the marketplace, they begin to *lather, rinse,* and *repeat* on those processes and subsequently stop learning new things. Eventually, they become in danger of becoming one-trick ponies, and the organization effectively stamps an expiration date upon its forehead and begins winding down.

But ambidextrous organizations behave differently. Organizations like Google, Toyota, Zappos, 3M Corporation, and others have adopted a different model. This model follows biology and principles like *negative entropy* (the breathing in and out of living organisms); it considers the principles and language of quantum physics as an operating language instead of just Newtonian physics and the industrialism from the turn of the last century. This model leverages the best of what the world and humanity currently offer, like *diversity, abundant and available knowledge, increased consciousness, heightened intuition,* and *advances in technology* and *science* instead of simply relying on what's been successful in the past and worked yesterday. What's the takeaway here regarding paradigms and unthinking? It is that these cognitive frameworks will serve us well as the unthinking mind intuitively knows the building blocks of each paradigm. If circumstances in your environment change, however, and the intuitive (unthinking) mind gives you a pinch, it's time to look for a new one and to listen and act.

Philosophies Underlying Paradigms

In the book *A Brief History of Thought,* Luc Ferry (pronounced fur-ree') discussed defining moments in Western philosophical thought that have dominated history and subsequently affected the world. These philosophies, and in one case a religion, have influenced our thoughts and activities, whether we give them daily conscious attention or not. Philosophies and faiths, such as *stoicism, humanism, postmodernism, Christianity, pragmatism,* and most recently *contemporary humanism,* all Google-able terms, influence our world-view (a comprehensive conception of the universe and humanity's relation to it). By virtue of this, our organization's philosophy and worldview are also formed. There may be nothing written or spoken about philosophies or worldviews around your company, but I assure you they're there. From the furniture in the lobby to the architecture of the building and the boss's Maserati, clues are everywhere regarding your company's views about work and life; pay attention to and notice them. The natural order and flow of ambidextrous organizations, ones that can both exploit and explore the marketplace, borrow the best from these philosophies and movements and closely follow the current philosophical thinking of the day, *contemporary humanism,* a philosophy Ferry says offers a compelling blend of all the best values that have come before.

With stoicism, created by the ancient Greeks, humanity was introduced to the idea of logical thought, control of emotions (developing indifference to both pleasure and pain), and a logical cosmic order to the universe, external to us and beyond our influence. Contentment and harmony could be achieved by following a universal path.

Next came Christianity, and the focus turned from the outside world to the inside. Order was embodied in a person, and humanity was introduced to freedom of choice and the idea we were transient and capable of change. The locus of control had shifted from external (out of our control) to internal (within our influence and control). Furthermore, Christianity, like other religions, espoused a focus on serving humanity as opposed to objects or things.

Next came the scientific revolution in the 16th and 17th centuries, and humanity was once again pulled back to ideas of universal truths and laws. External control that was out of our hands, insignificance, and impermanence in a big world and even bigger vastness of space must have been an unfathomable and terrifying thought to many.

Perhaps to counter this, the philosophy of *humanism* came on the scene. Philosopher Jean-Jacques Rousseau set out to reinterpret the scientific revolution with man at the center, having dominion over, or at least control of himself within its mechanical workings.

With each philosophy or belief, the pendulum seems to swing between a rational (logical) and normative (behavioral) approach and between an exploitative (narrowly focusing) and explorative (broadly expanding) focus and thought in a sine wave pattern. Two rational traditions worthy of note are pragmatism and *post-modernism*. Pragmatism emphasizes practical application. In 1907, William James, Harvard professor, said pragmatism was perhaps America's greatest contribution to the world. Frederick Nietzsche, German philosopher and architect of the *postmodern era,* taught that focusing on the "here and now" was of the most importance; focusing thought on anything else was a waste of time.

Ambidextrous organizations borrow the best from the ebb and flow of each of the philosophies and faiths. One reason is because these organizations are more in sync with the complexity of life.

Contemporary Humanism and Ambidexterity

Just like structures, values can be vertical or horizontal. The philosophies discussed above are compilations of beliefs, and each forms structures that either spread horizontally across humanity or build up vertically in columns of specific (disassociated from humanity) activities, disciplines, and thought. Borrowing from the best in stoicism, Christianity, pragmatism, postmodernism, and particularly humanism, philosophers have rethought humanism to arrive at *contemporary humanism,* a new philosophy that incorporates logical rationality and defines spirituality in nonreligious ways for both work and life.

One of the ideas of the new contemporary humanist movement is transcendence. The concept comes from postmodern thinking and is illustrated by German philosopher Edmund Husserl and his matchbox analogy. We know that a matchbox has six sides, but when it is held up to our eyes, we can see only three sides at a time; the other sides of the box are hidden from view, though we conclude they are there. For Husserl, this suggested something interesting: that some things are transcendent, beyond our knowing. Some parts of reality are unknown; we automatically fill in blank spaces with our minds in the models we build for utility and convenience. While not everything is seen, it is important to acknowledge these unknown parts.

This is the way that mental models like paradigms and schema serve us best. They serve as servants for us, building bridges and connections from the known to the unknown and identifying the parts still under construction, rather than serving as masters telling us unequivocally what is. Ambidextrous organizations operate in the same way. Whether companies are currently exploiting or exploring in the environment, they never assume unseen portions of a business are as they were yesterday. Consequently, they test reality with the belief that some things are transcendental and prone to change. Though we may be able to mentally configure a complete reality with confidence from what we can see, that doesn't mean it's concrete. A great many yet unknown details can and do end up being filled in prematurely. Once we become comfortable with the idea that we can never see all our reality at once from our sole and unique perspective, we can train our minds to a new definition of reality that includes an element of the unknown and unseen for exploration.

Under our new definition and paradigm, the presence of one thing implies the absence of something else, and this should be sought out and considered. Under our old paradigm, we would have likely ignored or overlooked such ideas. Reality depends on angle of observation; whichever angle we use to view life will inform our real and transcendental experience.

Husserl taught us that no matter how we contemplate reality, we can never totally grasp it, and we cannot totally grasp it alone. Ambidextrous organizations have learned that *shared* explorative practices combined with focused exploitation enable them to perform at peak efficiency, imagine more, and shine light into corners individuals alone cannot illuminate.

Husserl's experiment also transfers into other notions like not assuming all perspectives are the same or that some are better (more valuable or advantageous) than others. Thought, reflection, and problem solving are not linear exercises. Allocation should be given for time, uncertainty, and figuring things out.

Active and Reactive Forces

Also from postmodernism comes Frederick Nietzsche's belief that the world is split into opposing *active* or *reactive* forces. According to Nietzsche, reactive forces function by denying and repressing other forces. This idea fits with established exploitative organizational practices designed to be followed, repeated, preserved, and protected as originally created. These represent a narrowing of prescribed behavior and thought in the name of efficiency and perfection. Think of a surgeon or aviator following critical checklist steps or a factory worker repeating steps in an assembly line, where if these procedures are not followed exactly the consequences could be dire or costly. Active forces, by comparison, don't repress other forces, in part because such forces are yet unknown. The focus is on discovery or creation. Active forces open new perspectives. When done right, they attempt to follow as few established pathways as possible.

Art and music come to mind as examples of experiences that do not need to prove any other predecessor wrong. For example, you could not say that Picasso was wrong, and Monet was right. The same idea holds true for free associative thought or any type of exploration, physical or mental. Such trailblazing activities often have little referential precedence, so there should be nothing to honor, oppose, or protect.

As with organizational ambidexterity, which embraces both exploitation and exploration, Nietzsche recommended working to balance action and reaction, a practice he called a "will to power" and achieving it "the grand style." This balanced, orchestrated dance is choreographed daily by ambidextrous and complexity leaders in the most innovative companies around the world.

Identifying Your Organization's Worldview

If you don't know your organization's philosophy and world-view, I encourage you to seek it out because the unthinking mind has both and will know, and let you know, if there is a culture clash. You may discover your company has never considered one. All the same, one or several of these philosophies are present. Is your organization more reason or faith based? For Christian-based businesses like Hobby Lobby or Chick-fil-A, it's relatively easy to tell their philosophies and worldviews, but not so for other organizations. Look in your company's tenets, value or mission statement, employee manual, or handbook, or ask the CEO. These are its *espoused values*, what it says is important. Is its worldview *normative* or *rational*, that is to say, are its processes of control organized along following set rules or employee empowerment? Is it ambidextrous (exploitative and explorative), and if so at what percentages—90% exploitative and 10% explorative? 60/40?

Beyond capitalism, humanism, or any other type of "ism," a company may endorse a base (unthinking) desire in all of us to learn, help, contribute, create, and exercise our brain and its "right" creative functions, its left logic cognitive functions, or both. How much and in what ways we can do this, and our company's views, may ultimately determine our happiness and success. To reconcile the unthinking mind, once you discover your organization's philosophy and worldview, reflect and ask yourself whether it aligns with yours, and whether or not that matters to you.

Starting Over and Finishing Complete

When important things in your environment change dramatically (like paradigms), you may find yourself in a "starting over" tailspin, but it doesn't have to be that way, and you don't have to start over if you're navigating with an *unthinking* open mindset. Ambidextrous (learning) organizations have a unique structure built on both a vertical and horizontal axis (like a cross), giving their organizations and their employees the freedom to think and act in a number of pivotal ways depending on the environment. In my book, *The Rise of the Ambidextrous Organization: The Secret Revolution Happening Right Under Your Nose,* I present a simple chaos structure model focused on vertical hierarchical structures and horizontal innovative structures and the mindsets that accompany each. Research into paradigm-changing technological innovation and companies that were either vertically or horizontally aligned structurally showed that those that were aligned vertically into the old technological paradigm had a difficult time exploiting the new innovation and paradigm, while those aligned horizontally adjusted effortlessly. The idea here is simple: This kind of cross-alignment model gives us the ability to pivot in both exploitive or explorative ways as the environment changes and gives us the ability to more intuitively unthink our way into a clear course of action. What follows are more tips, theories, and models to help you intuitively unthink your way to sustained success.

Jerry Colonna, author of *Reboot,* said that now more than ever, there are "ghosts in the machine"—things that are neither known, expected, or that we readily know what to do about. Knowing that we are finite, messy, asymmetrical beings and life is not a linear progression, we should be comfortable embracing *not* knowing at work (and life) and do the best we can every day without stressing too much about it.

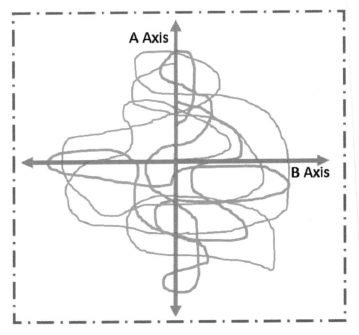

A Axis

B Axis

The Ambidextrous Chaos Model (Zabiegalski, 2018)

What does Colonna prescribe in order to cope with a messy changing kaleidoscope world? Once you know more about your philosophy and worldview and that of your organization, try some of these tips from Jerry's book and your life should get smoother and more fulfilling.

- Apply the logic of the do-over like when you were a kid. Activities might take iterations before they're right.

- Shoot, or learn to live with, your crow of self-criticism that endlessly caws at you when you think something hasn't gone exactly right. Although it is critical of you, it's also a part of you that cares, so you may want to reckon with it.

- Develop discipline and mental toughness, and they will be your champions in exploitative endeavors and defensive tackle during explorative ones.

- As Milarepa, a 10th-century Buddhist saint, said, "Surrender to your demons." By facing your fears head on, the reward is your freedom.

Field Theory: Understanding the Game

Field theory, structuration, and *habitus* may be foreign concepts to you, but they represent the simple idea that organizations and social groups are like soccer or football teams on a field of play. Do you know the mechanics of what's happening in your organization every day—the interplay, connections, and relationships? Would you like to know? If you answered yes, you're in luck.

A model I compiled from the works of Anthony Giddens, Kurt Lewin, Pierre Bourdieu, and Edgar Schein illustrates how organizations and individuals interact on a field of play to change one another. The concept goes like this: As agents (organizational members) enter a field of play (the organization), they interact with other players on the field. During their activities they act out scripts (behavioral patterns), written partially by the organization, partially by their interactions with others, and partially by the players. They affect and are affected by these exchanges on the field, and this ultimately becomes part of both an action realm of organizational activity as well as an institutional realm of collected knowledge.

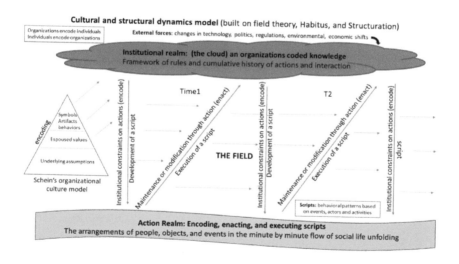

At the same time players (employees) are contributing to the action realm, they are also receiving from and contributing to an institutional realm, a realm of codified knowledge accumulated by the organization (top and bottom of the diagram). This institutional realm can be thought of as a *cloud* of knowledge collected by the organization in the form of norms, data, practices, stories, beliefs, etc.

Why is this important to know and consider? First, it's important because this kind of learning goes into the vast storehouse of the subconscious to be intuitively retrieved (remembered) later. Next, this ongoing exchange says something important about structure and learning. Namely, agents, their institutions, and the play field act as stressors and influencers upon one another, either challenging and modifying or supporting and reinforcing the current organizational structure. They're complex, unpredictable, and not entirely known until it's all over. Proof of this can be found in the idea that as these agents contribute to the accumulated codified knowledge of the organization and interact with others on the field while executing scripts, this execution of scripts does not always involve awareness or intentionality. Actors may simply behave according to their perception of the way things are. The ultimate enactment of a script will be partially known and partially unknown by those on the field and not "completely" known until it has played out. The actors change the script with their interaction with others and the environment.

Studying diagrams like this also promotes something called "meta learning." Simply put, meta learning means learning how to learn. Diagrams, concepts, maps, and models give us a big-picture understanding and promote meta learning. Meta learning helps us learn how to look for the big picture first, before drilling down to details; it's a way to set a structure or plan for learning and subsequently build strategies and achieve deep knowledge of a subject—skills that normally take years to develop. Getting in the habit of starting with a meta learning approach, studying the big picture before rushing onto the field, is a better strategy for getting to a deep understanding quickly and tucking that learning away into the subconscious of an unthinking mind. And diagrams, models, maps, and concepts are some of the very best ways to meta learn.

Players on the Field: Jackrabbits and Slow Learners

Now that I've introduced you to the idea of field theory, let's look at the two main types of players (learners) on the field and how they dramatically influence performance.

Around 1975, researcher Robert Duncan came up with the concept of organizational ambidexterity after noticing that many of the best organizations practiced what he called "switching rules" and periodically switched between exploitative (getting their "bread and butter" normal work done) and explorative (being creative, innovative, and thinking of "out-of-the-box" new ideas) behavior. In 1981, James March came along and turbocharged Duncan's work by introducing *learning* to the concept. When this happened, the floodgates on ambidexterity opened. More scholars began to make contributions, introducing ideas like evolutionary learning, revolutionary learning, radical and punctuated learning, and intentionally perturbing, or "shaking up" learning. This is when things began to really get exciting!

One of March's ideas is particularly intriguing and resonates with virtually all of the adult students and business professionals I talk to. It is the idea of *fast and slow learners* in the workplace. We often have skewed perspectives of both and the contributions they make, and this idea has caused many to take account of and look more closely at what is going on under the hood of their organizations.

Let's call the fast learners jackrabbits. Within each organization, there is an accumulated wealth of knowledge we call the organizational code. Think of the code like a cloud of learned practices, knowledge, and behavior floating above the organization— everything the organization learns and knows is there, the stories, techniques, processes, data, etc. In the course of daily work, members act and interact on the playing field of business, and in the course of this work they take from and contribute to this codified accumulated company knowledge.

March discovered something remarkable: Slow learners contributed far more to the cumulative knowledge bank of the organization. The fast learners often contributed little to nothing while taking knowledge from the code. This is shocking considering that fast learners are often celebrated and lauded as high performers and rewarded with freer reign, more autonomy, and higher pay, while slow learners are seen as underperforming, undesirable, and detrimental, often being demoted, restricted, micromanaged, or dismissed. The varied treatment of fast and slow learners sends a troubling message to the organization's gritty learners and conscientious mistake makers regarding the value of learning, sharing, and communication. In defense of our organizational jackrabbits, however, they may not mean harm or intend to behave selfishly; they may simply be predisposed to moving fast, working alone, and not sharing. There's a good chance they don't see their lack of contribution to the team or are supported by leadership.

Akin to the ideas in Daniel Kahneman's great 2011 book *Thinking Fast and Slow,* in which Kahneman said we think in two ways (fast or slow), we additionally learn along this same dichotomy. Both types of thinking, and learning, are required in organizations for healthy, sustainable performance and growth, and we must strive to understand the purpose and value of each. From the newest person in the organization to the CEO, it's up to all of us to help everyone play their best game!

Diversity and Workplace Relationships

There's a lot of talk of diversity these days, but it's largely ignored, misunderstood, and subconsciously feared. For many, diversity equals chaos and *that* is to be avoided at all costs. It's dangerous and there isn't time for people, environments, or activities that are not laser focused on objectives. Yet study after study, as well as seminars, science, and stories have shown that diversity is one of the major keys to sustainable success, if not the most important thing. So what are we getting wrong or not doing in creating and nurturing healthy productive diversity? The answer is *coherent diversity.*

The first time I thought about the concept of diversity in organizations and business, it was in the context of ethnic diversity. While this is certainly important and valuable, it's not the only thing/ You're not done if you simply, superficially, hire people of different ethnicities. That is just one component, one expression of human diversity, albeit an easily visible and discernible one. We can see people of other colors, people with different accents, speaking different languages, and we can observe other cultures and gather hints of potentially different belief systems within them. Diversity done wrong can feel like the destructive and crazy chaos we fear most, so what's coherent diversity?

What if we were to bake a cake and bought everything necessary—eggs, flour, yeast, frosting, sprinkles. After we gathered the ingredients and left them on the counter, they probably wouldn't manifest into a cake. They would stay individualized in the forms they were. So, what if we then took action by taking the eggs and smashing them on our heads, shaking the flour all over ourselves, swallowing the yeast, and smearing the frosting on our face. Would we have a cake at the end, or a ridiculous mess? What I'm trying to say is that coherent diversity is like making a cake. It's the logical ordering and assemblage of all possible and different expressions of human diversity in the environment—cognitive, experiential, and natural characteristics and not simply the ones that are most pervasive like color or gender.

Never Throw Anyone Off the Bus

The bus is a metaphor for workplace inclusion, diversity, psychological safety, and most especially learning. We should *never* throw anyone off the bus. Hopefully, you think of your workplace like a school bus of learning and think of the other riders as your classmates in this journey of growth, change, and ever-increasing discovery and performance.

That said, internal competition, protectionism, and even occasional thuggery occur in the workplace and appear to be on the rise. We routinely exclude each other from workplace learning, kicking others off the bus and sometimes off the team, department, or the organization entirely. We abandon, deny, neglect, and shun, all the while hunkering down and protecting ourselves and our positions. It's the opposite of a learning environment, or, if we're learning anything, it's how to survive and be shrewdly cautious.

Behavior like this may produce results in performance for those who are adept at individual competition, but other valuable members who want to contribute shrink and fall away. I can assure you any perceived wins are tactical (short term) and not group strategic wins if they're wins at all.

One danger in this inadvertent fragmentation of the workforce is the grave effect it has on culture, leaving you with only those who have learned to embrace a mercenary ethos, work alone or in temporary advantageous alliances, and primarily work for money, extrinsic reward, and ultimately themselves. This business operating system entraps members, beguiles leaders, and weaves its tentacles through an organization's body, using communication (or lack of it) and observed behavior to slowly cripple and calcify an organization. What you will likely be left with is a company of bullies and hit men, calculating tacticians, and shortsighted aloof leaders.

Another problem with such an operating system is that when highly competitive individuals run out of non–like-minded people to occupy their suspicions, they set their sights on one another until the workplace comprises either all the same people or a company of three (you, the current winner, and their competitor), and they will eventually form a temporary alliance and come gunning for you. Let's look at things you can do to keep everyone on the bus, retain a diverse workforce, quell difficult people and help with their challenges, and ensure your culture stays healthy and your workers feel safe. What do things like acceptance and embracing diversity and inclusion have to do with thinking intuitively, unthinking? Plenty.

Realize Everyone Does Something Important

Some people are product makers, some are process helpers, and some do both. Sometimes we make things, and sometimes we make things better, and making things better is just as valuable as making something tangible. Commercials that ran in the 1990s for a company called BASF stated, "At BASF we don't make a lot of the products you buy; we make a lot of the products you buy, better. BASF, the spirit of innovation." This subtle yet significant statement is right: sometimes we improve upon existing processes, procedures, and products or shepherd them along, and this can make all the difference.

Recently, I heard a new expression from a friend: "Seam-SME." While I haven't had the opportunity to ask them what it meant, I assume it is a subject matter expert who can connect and integrate concepts or products together, revealing a bigger picture. If so, this is a great sign. Polymaths, generalists, and 21st century renaissance men and women who are an "inch deep and a mile wide" in experience are making a strong comeback after centuries of being dismissed in favor of specialists and niche experts. Thank goodness for that—they're needed! Here's a foot stomp regarding high "generally experienced" people and unthinking behavior. They have often moved so much specific and technical knowledge to the subconscious mind that their presence on a team is invaluable.

Recognize Your Ability to Show Up

In the 2001 movie *Hardball*, Keanu Reeves coaches at-risk inner-city youths who often have trouble doing the simplest of things like getting themselves to practice due to difficult circumstances at home and in their communities. What is Reeves commentary to them when this problem hits a climax and the kids lose their last bit of hope? "I'm blown away by your ability to show up!" he tells them.

Sometimes we need to be blown away by others' ability to show up with their game face on. We need to apply empathy to others, and ourselves, when we are not at our best. People have up and down days, feel high and low energy, and experience focus and diffusion depending on current circumstances. When this happens, it's not the time to pounce, cut in line, step over them, or deliver a mortal blow; it's the time to draw on empathy and rally for them. Sometimes showing up is everything, the most important thing, and what matters. Motivational speaker Jack Canfield said, "Treat every relationship like you're responsible for 100% of it"; that way, when the other person is giving less than 50%, you can pick up the slack!

Call Out Collusion and Deceitful Discourse

Successfully innovative organizations communicate with knowledge, and they do it in inclusive ways. They use knowledge sharing vs knowledge control or knowledge management. I suppose each has a place in the organization if we talk in terms of specificity. However, problems arise when we (collectively or individually) default to the last two forms of communication unnecessarily, like if we don't have the stomach for it, or we tactically use knowledge management or control with an agenda or intent other than that of the group and its objective. When we switch modes of communication or attempt to control the message, at worst we collude and deceive. However you justify it, it raises questions and can taint culture and relationships. Call it out whenever possible.

Be a Helper and Put Others First

Forget about the TPS reports for a minute (a 1999 "Office Space" movie reference) and consider what children's television show host Mr. Rogers might do in the office. Educator Fred Rogers once said, "The worst thing a person can do to another is diminish them." This is a truth I strongly believe, yet we literally, inadvertently, diminish others nonstop in our workday lives. Do you think I'm exaggerating or being melodramatic? I'm not and could prove it but I won't; I'll leave you to reflect on your daily and weekly interactions with others.

How do we diminish one another? We do it in subtle yet damaging ways by not including others, not listening, behaving carelessly, and making judgments and disparaging remarks. The micro-disrespect we inflict mostly goes unnoticed but leaves a residue. I've always liked the saying, "Go where you're celebrated and not tolerated." Perhaps there's another alternative. Perhaps we can create a workplace in which everyone is celebrated, and no one is relegated to tolerance. I believe Fred Rogers' statement and would add that our first job in life should be to encourage one another daily to reach for the sun.

Slow Down Your Jack Rabbits and Give Your Turtles Jetpacks

The previous chapter discussed the concept of fast and slow learners. I've worked with a lot of brilliant engineers and other specialized professionals who were uber smart in very specific subjects, but not every subject. Collaborating and contributing to others' learning success was usually not on their priority list. In their minds, if you couldn't keep up with what they were currently focusing on, perhaps you needed to find another profession. If we can slow down our fast learners, like our brilliant engineers, and instill in them the hearts of teachers, as well as celebrate and support our slow learners, it could go a long way to creating an amazing productive culture.

Seek Self-Improvement

Despite whatever reality you may be experiencing, keep working on you and be relentless about improving. Keep your "double-loop learning" feedback loops turning all the time; put them on autopilot so they run automatically.

What is double-loop learning? It's a type of learning that involves action, reflection on outcomes, and modification of behavior the next time you act. I'm not prescribing continually flogging yourself with self-criticism. What I am suggesting, however, is to never stop questioning and looking at what you did, asking how it went, what you'll do differently next time, and how you could do it better. Be relentless in this self-improvement and privately exhaust yourself in it. But don't let anyone else know; it's none of their business. Put this advice into your crosschecks and it will serve you well.

Understand the Importance of Culture

Jack Welsh, the past CEO of GE, said culture is the most important thing. In the book *No Bullshit Leadership*, Chris Hirst told the story of Welsh's two questions to help you determine which employees are holding your company back: "First, does an employee fit in with the culture of your organization? Second, do they deliver results?" If the answer is yes to both questions, they're obviously a great fit, and those who don't get the culture and don't deliver need to be let go. But here's the interesting part. Employees who get your company's culture but don't deliver need to be retained, because according to Welch, "culture is paramount." They should be assigned a coach to improve performance. And what about those who deliver results but don't fit with the culture you're trying to establish? Welsh believed these employees restricted cultural growth and hampered their teams and their organizations. He recommended letting them go.

Furthermore, Welsh said diversity always wins. "You'll need a mix of dependable professionals and unpredictable mavericks," as well as ethnic, cognitive, experiential, gender, and age diversity. Homogenous teams look attractive, get along well, and are easier to lead. However, like-minded, like-acting people arrive at premature watered-down solutions borne of groupthink.

The humanistic, social side of culture is the hardest part to get our heads around and the least valued. It's difficult for companies to figure out when they would rather focus energy on things like stocking cans on shelves, logistics, and the objective scientific processes related to the production of things. Activities like getting people to learn in optimal ways, focusing on caring for one another, or making employees feel happy and secure (which ironically would make them more productive and increase performance) are difficult and not as valued.

Recently while reading the news I came across lists of the 101 highest-paying college degrees followed by the 50 lowest-paying college degrees. On the highest-paying list, 92 jobs had the word "engineer," "math," "economics," "science," or "management" in the title; among the lowest-paying degrees, 46 had the words "human," "health," "social," "community," "children," "education," "art and culture," or "outdoors" in their titles. The message here is clear: left-brained, quantifiable, objective, tangible, non–human-centric careers are king, paying the most, while jobs focusing on the development of people, serving humanity, or dealing with intangibles are not. What does this mean for you and for unthinking? If you're a left brain–disposed person, you're most likely in that lucky cohort of highest-paid earners, so that's good, but you might also be at a disadvantage when it comes to unthinking. Right hemisphere thinkers, by comparison—while routinely making less money because they're more interested in humanity, the human side of enterprise, and an embodied living world enacted with and viewed in context vs the creation of "things"—are more aware and tapped into intuition and the subconscious mind. Imagine if you had easy command of and a pipeline to both the left and right hemisphere of the mind.

Open the Aperture of Reality

So why do we kick people off the bus? It's complicated but much of it has to do with the way each of us sees reality. These perceptions are complex and can be *very* different from one person to another. In his book *Metahuman*, Deepak Chopra said, "Our day-to-day reality is inauthentic and compromised by the limiting mental and social frameworks that we impose upon it." And we impose a lot. There is a meta reality (a reality beyond the layered identity we create) that exists outside of the interpretations that humans add, and it's extremely difficult to get to. Our mind-made reality doesn't just comprise all the data that gets filtered through our senses; it's also made up of the ideas and impressions we filter through a complex matrix of beliefs.

Chopra went on to say, "We persistently translate immaterial concepts into material forms; tangible, physical concrete things." Anything that manifests in the material world—a shirt button, a painting, an automobile—first started in the mind of an individual. We then celebrate, attend to, and hold on high our creations (what we have manifested). That's why office spreadsheets become so important, and why the highest-paying jobs in the world deal with the creation, and creators, of concrete tangible things.

The uncomfortable (and wonderful) truth is that we are constantly changing transient beings, but we assign fixed characteristics to one another and ourselves rather than considering new possibilities and our propensity to change, learn, and grow. While locking identities down may help us cope, it also limits potential, and we get caught in a tangled network of beliefs, social frameworks, mental conditioning, experiences, and opinions. Like the things we physically manifest, our sense of self also becomes *reified* (converted into a concrete thing), and when we do this, we deny ourselves of our true infinite potential and delimit and descope others and ourselves. Perhaps there is no place where this is done more often than in the workplace.

Climate and Culture: Doing the Work We Love, and Sometimes Hate to Do

Your organization's climate is determined by its culture; it quantifies the culture's *beliefs, values,* and *assumptions* and expresses its meaning. What is climate? On the surface, it's the general mood of your workplace. Think of it like the daily weather conditions in the office. A healthy climate has a *value orientation,* and there are four categories: *rule oriented, people oriented, goal oriented,* and *innovation oriented.* The values of the organization's culture should determine this orientation.

Here's an example of value orientation. If you work in the crab fishing industry or the aviation industry (two dangerous professions), then your business culture most likely values rules above all else; you are a *rule-oriented* culture. If on the other hand you are in the business of producing and fielding products or services, your culture is most likely *goal oriented.* If you are creating and fielding innovative products, you could be both *goal* and *innovation* oriented. You get the idea.

Organizations often get themselves into trouble when they don't state and transmit their culture's value orientation to their members, and this affects both their climate and their culture. To use our weather metaphor, your workforce may never be quite sure what the weather will be on any given day, as individual members will prioritize different values based on their personal preferences and perspective, which may clash with others in the organization. A lack of clear guidance from leadership regarding what organizational values apply can thrust members into chaos and confusion. At the very least, backing the wrong values is confusing and frustrating; it could even get you fired if you double-down on what you value most. At the very worst, you could get injured or killed if you're not following the rules in a dangerous profession.

Incongruence in cultural values is one of the chief reasons organizations experience troublesome climates without ever being sure why. This is a problem that is difficult to diagnose and chase down. Like phantom flu symptoms you just can't shake, it hangs on and is nondescript. Things should be running more smoothly, and people should be working together more harmoniously, but you can't put your finger on why they're not.

Organizations can be complex places. We often need to focus on prioritizing more than one value and relay these clearly to our workforce. Making them understand what each one is, why it's important, and where it fits in the "rack and stack" of your company's value priorities is the job of leaders. We've all heard the metaphor of the "rudderless ship," blowing whichever way the wind takes the sails instead of being steered. This ship eventually breaks apart when it encounters rocks. However, this cautionary tale is probably more akin to a ship with a malfunctioning rudder than a missing one, working at some times but not at others. On-again, off-again cultural values express their indifference through your climate. You're left with a trading floor of oft-clashing people trying to get through the day focusing on what they think is important or needed, based on their personal value orientations. What's the potential impact on unthinking processes here? The intuitive unthinking mind of the right hemisphere never gets an opportunity to do what it does best, to operate optimally in an embodied contextual world, because it is constantly under siege and exercising fight or flight in one survival scenario after another.

Getting Back on Course

How do we get back on course? The answer is with a functioning rudder (a culture) that is steering all the time in known (stated) orientations and in weather (a climate) that projects consistent expected patterns. It's quite simple to achieve and have this once you understand and get the hang of it. The difference to remember is that bad and unexpected weather will come and go, but it will be *external* to your organization, not *internal*. With a culture defined and tended by a caring leader, the organization will be trained for any weather, know what to do, and be empowered and focused when it comes in.

This is a leader's job, but it is also a manager's job, a worker's job, everyone's job. Each of us have an important role regardless of our crew position aboard ship. When bad weather comes, regardless of whether the organization chooses to sail towards it or it's unexpected, people who are motivated become handy in shifting winds. But motivated people who also understand and stand behind the organization's culture will be invaluable in the event of a shipwreck.

Listen, Watch, Reflect, and Then Act

The final part of getting back on course and helping others do the same involves checking and understanding our own bearings and their limits. Humans are flawed beings, so any rules made will also contain flaws. Nothing is perfect so expect, accept, and embrace imperfection as part of the beauty of life. Question and evaluate values and processes and see if logically (and ethically) they make sense and if they need updating or refining. A logical view of reality is centered on reasonableness, but that doesn't mean it's objective. As psychiatrist Lain McGilchrist said, "Even rationality is grounded in intuition. You can't rationally prove that rationality is a good way to look at the world. We simply "intuit" that it's best."

It's also never possible to experience objective reality; our minds don't work that way. The closest we can come is through the right hemisphere of the brain, but it quickly becomes modified. At last count, psychologists identified 188 biases of the mind, and these in turn support a multitude of daily assumptions. As a big filter, the brain works hard to see patterns and order often random things into logical order. The daily reality we experience is essentially a simulation created by the brain with a great many variables. Think about that the next time you're at work.

Finally, there will always be an element of life and experience that is unknown to us—unseen and unforeseeable. What this means operationally is that we shouldn't rush to judgment, interfere with otherwise self-correcting processes, take away another's freedom of choice or self-efficacy, or make a final decision until we absolutely have to. The universe may reveal a helpful part of the picture previously hidden from view if we wait.

All we have control over is our own thoughts, feelings, and actions, so let's operate from there. As someone once said, "It's not what happens to you in life that matters; it's how you react to it." You will encounter all manner of weather in life. Make your daily forecast (your climate) a beautiful and pleasant sunny day.

Storytelling and Indigenous Wisdom for Business

A few years ago, I had a remarkable experience. I was invited to present research at a unique conference held, the year I attended, on the campus of the New Mexico State University. The conference, known as the Quantum Storytelling Conference, is hosted by Dr. Grace Ann Rosile and Dr. David Boje. While it is primarily a conference on storytelling in organizations, it carries a dual theme of examining Indigenous ways of knowing (IWOK) and Western ways of knowing (WWOK) in business.

The conference reminded me of a series of conferences from the mid-1980s held at the Santa Fe Institute in which scientists from diverse disciplines gathered to discuss common questions and challenges. The result was the birth of complexity science in business. Complex adaptive systems and organizational complexity are constructs taken from other disciplines that are just now being seriously applied in business to understand, explain, and improve our diverse, fast-paced, continually changing world.

Like those game-changing meetings in Santa Fe, the quantum storytelling conference is also attended by people with diverse backgrounds. Scientists, engineers, anthropologists, sociologists, biologists, linguists, artists, musicians, authors, poets, educators, strategists, environmentalists, and business professionals gather to discuss subjects such as sustainable business strategies, integration, corporate social responsibility, communication, humanity, and ecology. The conference is international, hosting people from several regions in Europe and the Middle East and attended by Indigenous peoples from the Americas (South, Central, and North to include Canada) and from New Zealand and Australia.

The research I presented was based on my recent book, *The Rise of the Ambidextrous Organization*, which addressed how today's

43

most innovative organizations have found a different, intuitive, and sustainable way of doing business. The approach is based on the natural cycles and rhythms of life and enlists the concepts of complexity, physics, biology, and human dynamics. To make a relevant contribution, I compared my research with *Tribal Wisdom for Business Ethics* written by Dr. Rosile and discussed how they complemented or contrasted with one another.

I was nervous going in. For one thing, I wasn't sure if my research complemented indigenous ways of knowing at all. Second, I wasn't sure if it would have anything new to say. Would people make a connection and make sense of my work, or would it be viewed as another superficial business idea, a gimmick?

What I came away with, however, was exciting and encouraging. It was the realization that organizational ambidexterity was a kind of "business bridge," connecting a newer progressive Western way of thinking (ambidexterity) with ancient Indigenous values and practices. The bridge spans a gap that has previously allowed ignorance and indifference to marginalize and ignore Indigenous business practices for centuries. Indigenous culture holds valuable lessons for national and global sustainability, building more meaningful and fulfilling workplaces, and living your best purposeful life. Perhaps most exciting was discovering that some of the biggest challenges WWOK currently struggle with and often get wrong are addressed by IWOK intuitively and effortlessly, incorporating principles of unthinking and the intuitive mind.

Modern-day organizations and businesses need to be exposed to these lessons now more than ever. As Einstein said, we can't solve the problems of tomorrow using the solutions of today; we need new approaches. While ancient Indigenous practices may not be new, they certainly are seldom considered in modern Western business.

What follows are *eight aspects of tribal wisdom* taken from *Tribal Wisdom for Business Ethics*. This, along with other stories from that trip, make up the latest discoveries to help architect a better world for everyone to live and work in.

Relationships vs. Transactions

The first aspect of tribal wisdom is the idea of building relationships above and beyond (and before) the transaction of business. Your initial knee jerk reaction might be, "Wait a minute. We don't always have time to get to know one another." I would beg to differ. Relationship building can happen in an instant, in a moment, and incrementally; it builds. It's established and set when we approach one another with a desire to be helpful, when we are open, observant, attentive, and respectful. This is not suggesting that you build a relationship for the sole purpose of transacting with them in order to negotiate more shrewdly or to outwit your opponent. To the contrary, it's suggesting that you make the relationship the "thing" you value and want instead of the other thing you want. Put this first and put the idea out of your head (at least momentarily) that there is something else you want from this encounter. Ultimately, conversation and activity will turn to the business at hand.

If possible, let them initiate the reason you're there, or, at the very least, wait until you feel as though their needs are met and they're ready to talk about business. By putting the individual first, attending to his or her needs and desire to be heard, and by establishing respect and trust, you clear a path for work to be done. Full attention can be focused on working together toward a mutually beneficial outcome.

Gifting vs. Getting

In Indigenous culture, a higher value is placed on giving than receiving. Indigenous members who consistently give in their communities are held in higher status, and in turn these individuals enjoy more social wealth. This contrasts with Western thinking, which celebrates amassing individual wealth and even hoarding. It wasn't long ago in the movie *Wall Street* that Michael Douglas spoke the words which have become a battle cry for over three decades: "Greed is good!"

Egalitarianism and Hierarchy

In her book *Tribal Wisdom for Business,* Grace Ann Rosile said the Euro-Western system of business is often viewed as warfare, described in battle and sports metaphors related to proving one's competitiveness and superiority over another. We language reality into existence. While there may be good justification to behave competitively with other companies when vying for market share, serious problems can arise when the focus is turned inward.

Furthermore, when considering external competitors, it may be wise to reflect on your worldview, perspective, and personal philosophy when considering war or warlike language. Do we live in a world of abundance or scarcity? Do we need to always destroy and eliminate our competitors, or is it smarter to sometimes collaborate with and help them in a spirit of unity and coexistence?

Egalitarianism also means the belief in the equality of all people, particularly in political, social, and economic ways. In many Indigenous cultures, members are shamed by their communities if they consider themselves "better" than others. Hierarchy of status is discouraged. In innovative companies like ambidextrous organizations, both vertical (hierarchical), and horizontal (organic) structures are established because the janitor sweeping the shop floor could come up with the company's next million-dollar idea when considered an equal. Their thoughts and passions are as valued as their mop bucket.

Material Acquisition

Tribal wisdom includes a lack of interest in the permanent acquisition of things. It's interesting how some people value relationships and experiences more than things, while others spend a lifetime acquiring "stuff." Furthermore, the same people who horde often "shed" their things, downsizing decades of acquisitions later in life.

There is a tie here to organizations. We often collect and acquire things in midlife. Call this boon conquest, efficiency, or validation, individuals seem to follow the same cycle businesses do—innocence, honesty, and inquisitiveness, followed by performance, shrewdness, and acquisitiveness, and ending with validation, attainment, and settling down into a life more defined by purpose than property. A personal life is not unlike a business's life; it's just a perspective of comparative scaling.

Usefulness

Akin to pragmatism, the law of usefulness says that if I'm going to own something, it will have a regular usefulness and purpose. This approach cuts down on acquisitiveness. You may have heard your father or grandfather ask, "Why do I need that? What would I use it for?" How often do you ask yourself that question?

Bartering

There's something inherently beguiling about money. The power of monetary symbolism on the human brain and psyche is perhaps one of the most alluring and pervasive things I've ever witnessed. It changes people in profound ways.

In a study conducted several years ago, two classrooms were set up with timed tests and a proctor administering the test. In one room, symbols of money, including coins, bills, and dollar signs, decorated the walls and computer screensavers. The other room had pictures of nature on the walls. An actor was hired to rush into the room late just as the test started and spill his or her books, papers, and pencils. In the room adorned with symbols of money, no one stopped to help the embattled test taker. In the room depicting nature, virtually all attendees either stopped to help or monitor the troubled person. For this reason, downplay money and minimize it in conversations and transactions for as long as possible.

Trust

I tell friends that I value three things in leaders: transparency, predictability, and fairness. Why, because together these things foster and convey trust.

I used to have a boss who, while being painfully challenged in the "great leader "category, did have one redeeming quality that kept him in the great boss department. He always parked in the same spot in the parking lot below my office window; he was predictable. It gave me a sense of comfort to know his patterns, and this in turn lowered my anxiety, allowing me to direct energy to the work at hand.

Trust among Indigenous people in business is a given; it's the norm, the default. In IWOK, you don't have to remind yourself to trust or strive to be trusted, and you don't have to be suspicious or wary. It may bewilder and confuse Indigenous persons if they were to encounter deceit, work with an untrustworthy person, or be cheated. They would likely become confused and not recognize what was happening. Does this make them naive or lacking?

As a member of Western business, individuals are occasionally judged by colleagues as "too nice," "too trusting," "naive," or "inexperienced." When this happens, are we really amateurs who are in over our heads, or do these accusatory words compensate for low character in an unnaturally corrupt environment?

Disclosure

Akin to trust, there's disclosure. Traditional Indigenous people who barter or sell will tell you up front everything that's wrong with what they offer, and they trust they will receive the same in return.

Storytelling at Work

At the heart of these discussions on tribal wisdom and relationships is storytelling. As old as humanity, storytelling introduces art and substance to life and work and enriches human experience. Though we seldom think of it in the context of work, we frequently hear stories with limited purpose and messages—cautionary tales, stories of prowess, excellence, or deception, and stories of struggle and strife. Generally, stories at work are not intended to teach or mentor; they're often a spontaneous and random means of venting, conveying experience, showing power, or entertaining.

For Indigenous people, stories are revered, purposeful, thoughtful, and deliberate. And to Grace Ann Rosile and her husband David Boje, storytelling is a powerful and transformative tool that's making a much-needed comeback in Western society.

Stories not only offer a different way of thinking about things, requiring different neural pathways to convey, but also empower us, allowing us to take ownership of them. We compare, contrast, complete, and add to a story, so that it ultimately becomes ours, part of us. Kaylynn Sullivan TwoTrees, one of the contributors to *Tribal Wisdom for Business Ethics*, instantly spun my perspective on its heels when she suggested that "while we are breathing, the trees are also breathing us." Stories have that kind of transformative power.

Achieving Triple Bottom Line Balance Through Storytelling

To call Dr. David Boje a tireless advocate for corporate ecology and responsible stewardship would be an understatement. He's also a master storyteller, professor emeritus at New Mexico State University, Bill Daniels Ethics Fellow, and past endowed Bank of America Professor of Management in Las Cruces. He has published over 120 journal articles and 17 books on business ethics, corporate responsibility, ecology, and storytelling. Inventor of the term *ante-narrative*, David says ante-narrative is the idea that there is always an earlier story, an origin story, which feeds into storytelling in an iterative cyclical process. David also introduced the world to a triadic theory of storytelling, an idea that the components, origins, and experiences that make up a story are a vital part of it—perhaps even more important than the final refined and polished glossy brochure we are ultimately shown.

When Dr. Boje talks about achieving a "triple bottom line," he's referring to *profit, people,* and *planet* (also called a 3BL model), and it is a form of corporate social responsibility. It's the idea that these three elements should be managed with processes, formulas, and procedures to allow a company to responsibly balance and achieve all of them. It sounds wonderful, but is it possible? David said that to date he has only known of one company in Denmark that operates a true working 3BL with formulas and metrics to back it up. Most companies, David said, participate in some form of what he calls "greenwash." With ecological whitewashing, glossing-over of status quo practices, and putting profit above people and the environment, these companies have no true working strategies for sustainability. Jens Larson of Old Friends Industries in Denmark said his country has the most ambitious climate law in the world, and several Danish companies arguably come close to achieving David's definition of the triple bottom line. Among them are Orsted Wind Energy, Novo Nordisk Pharma, Maersk Shipping, and Danfoss.

In addition to being an iconoclast, David is an equal opportunity disrupter. He's as comfortable holding up a mirror to his own university and challenging it to live the triple bottom line as he is in taking on a multinational corporation. Whether he's teaching barefoot, protesting the abuse of sweatshops or sporting a suit and tie, David's focus and quest is balance and sustainability.

As discussed earlier, the cool thing about storytelling is that it allows personal ownership and organizational growth starting from the individual level. A story told, especially one that incorporates quantum elements like Indigenous storytelling does, is a multiplier, producing a potential for payout much higher than any checklist or written procedure could hope for. Such documents are valuable tools, but having them in place and rigidly enforced in critical fields like aviation and medicine can also be delimiting and even detrimental procedurally. When not accompanied with storytelling and other relational interactions, they allow no room for interpretation, ownership, change, or connection. On their own, they can rob individuals of independent thought, initiative, and ultimately motivation. These are areas where unthinking and tapping into the vast storehouse of the subconscious mind pays dividends. The underlying message in a "checklist-only" atmosphere is clear: You're less inclined to think and more encouraged to do as you're told. In too many organizations, people are hired for their hands and not their hearts or their minds. Most of us would gladly give all three and more if only asked.

Making Wisdom Chic and Climbing the Knowledge Ladder

What did I contribute to the Quantum Storytelling conference? I'm still running that question through my head. But there was one contribution that caught the attention of Dr. Don Pepion, tribal elder of the Blackfeet tribe and professor emeritus at New Mexico State University, of IWOK and quantum science. It was a diagram I created I called the knowledge scale (see below). Here's how it works.

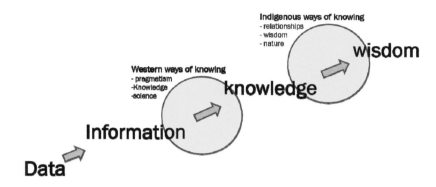

If we consider the act of "knowing" we can visualize an ascending line from left to right consisting of "data," "information," "knowledge," and finally "wisdom." Today, we are awash with data, and when put together it makes information. We use this information strung together to arrive at knowledge, and when we use knowledge in efficient, comprehensive, strategic, and altruistic ways, we can derive wisdom from it. When comparing IWOK to WWOK, I found that Indigenous people arrived at wisdom more often and more quickly than their Western counterparts. Why? I don't know definitively, but I think it may have to do in part with the practice of storytelling, the use of ritual and ceremony, the emphasis on relationships, a healthy caution toward symbols (like money) and acquisitiveness (the collecting of stuff), and an open intuitive (unthinking) connection with the natural world. Perhaps the next time I update this model I should include the learned behavior of "unthinking" somewhere between knowledge and wisdom.

Discovering Meta Reality

The photo below is George Mendoza, an artist I met while at the Quantum Storytelling conference, who sees the world in a unique way. George is blind. Much like Van Gogh saw the world with hues of halos and swirls around objects, George has a rare form of blindness that causes him to see the world as swirls of bright colors and undefined shapes. George calls this an ability, his "Kaleidoscope eyes."

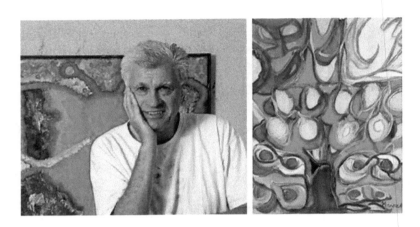

Earlier I discussed a meta reality beyond our everyday world—a truer reality above the one we live in, with all that has defined us and all we have accumulated stripped away. Layers collected over decades of experiences as well as opinions, circumstances, and actions define, bound, and border who we become. The true meta reality of "us" is the original clear spring we originate from vs the muddy, overgrown delta we ultimately are after years of living. If we could strip away the vegetation, wash away the dirt, filter out the sediment and toxins, and remove the distractions, we would see more clearly what we are at our core.

George has achieved this to a degree not experienced by most, not by choice but by chance. Without the often-overwhelming distraction of sight, I would venture to say George understands more about himself than we do of ourselves. He understands behavior through sound and inflection, smell, touch, the feelings of the elements on his skin, and of course his amazing kaleidoscope sight.

Like all of us, George also lives a second, cognitive reality inside his head. However, while our inner world is most often subordinate to the outer world we are continually bombarded with through vision, I imagine in George's world the order may be flipped. From George's perspective, the outside reality he lives is secondary and the inside world of his thoughts and mind is primary. In some ways, this gives him the distinct advantage of a closer picture of a meta reality. Motivational coach Bob Proctor once said we have it all wrong: "We let the outside world control the inside when it should be the other way around." George also has an indomitable spirit; did I mention he won the Paralympics twice for long-distance running in track and field in the 1980s? He finished fourth in the 1500-meter race in Holland in 1980 and fourth again in 1984 in the 1500-meter race in New York. He also set the world record for fastest blind runner with a 4:28 mile and the national record for the half-mile at 2:10. George began long-distance running as a teenager, often running 100 miles a week to burn off his adolescent energy and frustration.

Being devoid of the distraction of conventional sight has perhaps brought George closer to his meta reality than you or I. What's the connection with George and unthinking besides meeting him at the Quantum Storytelling conference? Perhaps it's George's story of expression and life fulfillment, his spirit, or perhaps it's his unique intuitive way of knowing, and seeing the world. In his lifetime, Van Gogh sold one painting. George has already blown that record out of the water. If you'd like to pick up one of George's creations, you can contact him at spiritmangeorge@gmail.com. I know you will hit it off like old friends and leave feeling invigorated.

Things You Can Do

What are the intuitive unthinking takeaways of this chapter? What can you do today, tomorrow, and next week to enrich your life and those of others? Here are a few tips.

Look for Ancient Wisdom in Your Own Backyard

In the mid-Atlantic region of North America where I live, there were once more than a dozen distinct Indigenous tribes with names such as Shawnee, Lenape, Accokeek, Piscataway, and others. Today these tribes are names of streets, towns, and places, but the descendants of these people still exist. Seek out these Indigenous communities and invite them to speak to your organization about their business practices and lessons and ask their advice. What would they say to your group if invited to share their wisdom?

There are also several high-tech native defense companies operating in my city with names such as Bowhead and Chugach. The only reason I know these companies are native owned is because I once lived in Alaska and know them as familiar native names and places. Research local Indigenous people, affiliations, and groups in your community and invite them to give a talk. Ask for business-related stories, advice, and presentations, and overlay this with your own company culture, tenets, and beliefs. Are there comparisons? Differences? You may learn something about yourself you didn't know before. A native friend who is a member of the Odawa Nation, D. J. Vanas, is a good place to start. He speaks professionally around the world and has some great TED and YouTube talks available for viewing. Regardless of where you live in America, from New York State to Florida, hidden wisdom is waiting to be discovered.

Seek Sustainability and Put People First

Sustainability, social accountability, the triple bottom line, and ethical and moral practices are on many people's minds today, and humanity is spending a lot of energy trying to figure out how to get these things right. Larry Merculief, Aleut native and public speaker, said there's an "inside society" or reverse society spoken of among natives in the north, and it's a troubling phenomenon. Merculief said, "The heart used to tell the mind what to do and now the mind tells the heart." He noted that this reversal was pushing the life support systems of our planet to the brink. Larry said that to turn this troubling trend around, we need to get out of our heads. We live in a society that believes intelligence comes only from logic and the brain. If we are to get off this self-destructive path, we also need to think intuitively. What Larry is instinctively touching on is knowledge passed down through generations of his people and scientifically known today—things like neural cells residing in the heart and the gut (stomach), which communicate with the brain to bring a clearer and truer picture of reality and the nature of things. These are some of the things that the learned practice of *unthinking* can repair and set back into operation.

In the book *What Matters Now*, Gary Hammel said, "Without ethics, we have nothing. Humans make mistakes." Capitalism is an ideology that brings extraordinary privileges, as Hammel noted, but if capitalism isn't based on and led by moral ethical principles, everyone loses. He went on to say that we should "kill bureaucratic structures." While I'm personally in favor of shaking up and testing structures that become too rigid, both structural and cultural, in order to see if they are still viable and needed, I wouldn't destroy vertical hierarchical chains all together. In organizational ambidexterity theory, both vertical and horizontal structures are present and necessary, and the trick is to know when and how to shift from one to the other. An unfortunate sign of rigidity is often seen when innovative companies that originally challenged the status quo begin to defend it, and questions suddenly are seen as adversarial.

A final piece of advice from Gary to stay innovative and avoid *rigor-mortis* was to not "*think to build*" but instead "*build to think.*" Constantly challenge the status quo, not by looking for big disruptive innovations but instead by looking for small innovative changes in the unspoken needs and desires of others. Finally, keep in mind that recognition and accomplishment are also currencies, not just money and other extrinsic rewards. Be empathetic. Treat others not as you would want to be treated but instead as they want to be treated. Ask them, if need be; they will likely appreciate the question.

Incorporate Aspects of Tribal Wisdom to Help You Make Sense of the World

In the book *Sensemaking*, Christian Madsbjerg said that there's thick data and thin data. What makes data thick? He said it's less about objective knowledge than it is about the context of coalesced data. To get a better sense of this, we need to consider the nature of knowledge. Madsbjerg explained that there are four types of knowledge. First, there is objective knowledge; this is the basis for science, and objective knowledge is universally true. Second, there's subjective knowledge. This is knowledge based on personal opinions and feelings. Third, there is shared knowledge, public and cultural; it's shared human experience. Last, there's sensory knowledge, often thought of as your "sixth sense." This knowledge is intuitive. Sensemaking, Madsbjerg explained, as its name implies, entails synthesizing all four types of knowledge without prioritizing any one over the others. That exercise only comes after immersion in a context by the experiencers. This is one of the keys to the mechanics of *unthinking*, and the path is found by allowing the intuitive right hemisphere of the mind to contribute what is known and seen in the subconscious to the left hemisphere of the brain and its navigational and actionable view.

Embrace the Suck

Many people think work and their jobs are miserable affairs, and largely they don't have to be. "Embrace the suck" is an expression that means to find something you like in the thing you don't like. Many young people today have never been blessed with the teaching experience of long-term drudgery, servitude, apprenticeship, or conscription, and for that reason they are at a significant disadvantage. They don't yet know what it's like to endure and conquer something with will, mental strength, and intestinal fortitude. Their mettle has never been tested in these ways and they don't know what they're capable of, how high they can go, or how much they could achieve. I worry for them, that such experiences might be what separates them from greater fulfillment.

Repeat Sustainable Activities

Something I may like or value may be sustainable for me (at least for a time) but not for others. The kind of repeatable sustainability I'm speaking of here is the kind that is repeatable at the highest levels, for your family, your community, humanity, the planet, everyone.

This concept may be best filed away in your subconscious, unthinking mind so you can see what answers surface tomorrow, next week, or next month. This is also one of those line-walking things you can do, between the personal and professional. We crash through work like bulls in a china shop, repeating unsustainable activities and destroying relationships and potential collaborations without even realizing it. Then we scratch our heads wondering why things aren't working out or vilify and label others as difficult when a change in our behavior could have been the key to success and happiness.

PART 2:
UNTHINKING EVERYDAY LIFE

Unthinking your everyday life is not unlike unthinking in business. In fact, it could be argued it's the same, only more personal and able to be tailored to your unique life. With ever increasing frequency, it feels like our modern life is becoming more complex, complicated, and difficult to navigate when by all accounts it should be (becoming) easier. Is this an illusion or reality? What's going on? As I alluded to a moment ago, the natural world of living organisms and the universe are complex. It's not necessarily that they are becoming more complex; these things have always been complex. It's more that we are becoming more aware of this complexity and doing our very best to meet it head on, understand it, tackle it for our own survival and comfort, and control it—and that's where the complications come in. While complexity is the realm of nature, the complicated is the realm of mankind. What's the difference?

When we step out of our boardrooms, factories, and workplaces and into a natural world like that of the wilderness, we largely step *out* of a complicated world of man's creation and into the *complex* world of nature. For example, a jet engine is complicated. Made of mechanical pieces, springs, bolts, gears, tubing, and wires, an engine can be disassembled, analyzed, reassembled, stopped, and started, and has definitive borders that make it what it is. But nature's different. Nature is complex. Weather systems are complex. Rivers, streams, biology, life (human life), organisms, and the universe are all examples of complex systems not of our creation. Complex systems, like a hurricane or tornado for example, don't have definitive borders; they have transitions, they're malleable and subject to change, and they're unpredictable. They cannot be taken apart and analyzed, reassembled, shut off, and set back into motion (turned back on again), and they can't be controlled. As in the examples of living organisms or the natural world, these are things also not created by us, not completely understood. They may not ever be completely understandable; there may be aspects about them we will never know. The next time we are in a manmade world like work, we would do well to remember that the creations of man are not complex, but instead complicated, and like every puzzle, they have a solution that an expert could solve, while man himself and the natural world are different and may not be as readily understood.

In this world, expertise and objectivity will only be realized when everyone and all associated things are considered, involved, and included in a "better" solution. In this world, the truest objectivity is *intersubjectivity*. When we hear others speak of manmade complications as complex but solvable, know that these confident assurances are likely contradictions, and we're not being completely honest or clear with ourselves. They are solvable when they're complicated, or, put another way, the complicated part of them may be easily figured out. Their complex side, however, may only be solved in approximation and in context of a living embodied world with others, or, perhaps not at all.

We human beings will never be one of man's complicated creations. Though we wear the complications of humanity around us, we are ultimately part of the universe's natural complexity, one that we may not fully understand or one that might even never be fully understandable. Perhaps herein lies the rub. It would be simple to say that when we're building a boat, plane, automobile, or an organization with others, we are dealing solely with the complicated (a puzzle), and that when we are encountering feelings or the weather, our thoughts, or unexplained behavior, we are encountering the complex. But these two balls are in play simultaneously; the complicated and the complex are intermingled. The rational (analysis), which is the brain's left hemisphere view of the world, and the intuitive (reasoning), which is the gut instinct side that is the right hemisphere's view, the two, and their perspectives, are seamless; it's often difficult to distinguish and separate them. The trick to learning to unthink in our everyday life is to identify *each* as we navigate these spaces of experience and process reality, addressing each appropriately. Let's look at some of the pitfalls and trappings of a complicated world we contrive from complexity, and I think you will intuitively (subconsciously) begin to realize and practice ways in which to simplify and declutter the complicated and accept, appreciate, and work with the complex.

The Arrogance of Ignorance:
Why the Excuse of Not Knowing
No Longer Works

I remember a movie years ago, a Clint Eastwood western I think, in which a Franciscan monk was telling a troubled young man, "Ignorance is not a sin, my son," attempting to comfort him for some egregious mistake he made. I've carried that mantra around with me ever since and occasionally pull it out when I need to console myself for some boneheaded mistake I've made. But was the friar right? Is ignorance guiltless? In my case it almost always wasn't (I usually knew what I should or shouldn't have done but didn't want to accept the answer), and I'm starting to think, for humanity's sake, we can no longer afford to give this kind of willful ignorance a pass.

Ignorance means a "lack of knowledge or information." That's innocent enough. There are plenty of things we don't know, and you are not at fault if you don't know something. But what if you don't care to know, don't try to know, or avoid knowing altogether? Again, it's probably no problem provided it only affects you; you're free to be as dumb as you'd like. After all, where do you think the term "blissfully ignorant" came from? We routinely engage in shutting off, shutting down, and not wanting to know about unpleasant things or potential problems. Furthermore, we get evolutionary help with this from our brain, which acts as a big filter and gap filler, taking in only necessary information and tailoring it or adding to it in such a way that we can make sense of it and efficiently use it without seizing up. It goes without saying that if we could take in all information available to us at once, we might experience a psychotic episode.

But, what if this "not knowing" hurts or impedes someone else, and you do know that? Now could you be cited for your indifference. That's precisely what's been happening. The problem with this, besides being quite unnatural as our brain wants to make connections with others, is that humanity won't move forward until we actively address and do something about it. What's going on? Why do so many people we meet, work with, and depend on seem to be hunkering down and stubbornly (and stupidly) digging in their heels and burying their heads in the sand like the proverbial ostrich?

There's something else going on today besides childish willful ignorance, something that's causing people to take sides, choose corners, and fearfully and unapologetically retreat to a place where they can defend off all attackers and wait out some imagined zombie apocalypse. I call this phenomenon *the arrogance of ignorance,* and it's a defiant protectionist posture and a learned behavior. It's a type of cynicism that fosters a general distrust in reality—and it's everywhere. The reasons why good people are turning a blind eye, pretending not to notice and care, and behaving cynically in an age of readily accessible information and relatively positive world changes is complicated and complex. But I'm convinced it's not voluntary. They don't want to do it and I believe people are being sold a bill of goods, conditioned. Let's look at some of the likely reasons and then discuss how we can fix these ills with the subconscious of an unthinking mind before they start to cause real damage to humanity.

Disconnected and Depressed

In the book *Lost Connections,* Johann Hari discussed the most common reasons why so many in our society experience a low-grade depression that never seems to cease. The reasons, he claimed, largely relate to difficult life circumstances that encourage us to disconnect. To cope, many adopt a willful ignorance toward themselves and others. Some of the disconnects Hari noted were a disconnect from meaningful work (loss of control, authority, and a sense of powerlessness) and a disconnect from others (loneliness). Disconnection can cause depression and in turn isolation, aloofness, and a disinterest and indifference toward life.

We also need to realize the silent war raging around us every day. It's a war for your attention and your very thoughts and consciousness. I'm willing to bet you're not even aware of it. Most of us end up as casualties in this war or prisoners to it, or we hunker down, unsure what to do or where to go next.

Manipulated and Played

A recent London ad campaign depicted a beautiful tan woman in a bathing suit and a slogan: "Are you beach body ready?" The campaign faced public criticism across Europe. Protesters responded with their own slogan, which they spray painted over the billboard: "Advertising shits in your head."

The public outcry was tied to a disconnect from meaningful values. Although our lives can be motivated by two types of values, advertising pushes us toward extrinsic values and discourages intrinsic values. Extrinsic values have been shown to make us more depressed and isolated (once the positive feeling of the new thing you've purchased wears off) and in the long run proves to be less rewarding. Intrinsic goals, on the other hand, which include helping others and developing yourself into a better person, last for a lifetime and build deep connections and meaning.

The irony is that in the United States, it is unlikely there would have been any public outcry or even notice of manipulation or threatened values. Americans simply would have absorbed the billboard's message, internalized it, and accepted the idea that they were not beach body ready and felt bad about themselves or worked silently and desperately to change their appearance.

Divided and Conquered

Something significant happened on a national scale a few years ago. It's likely many missed it, but they didn't miss the effect it has had on them. For the first time in decades, a political candidate ran on a platform that suggested moving into the past instead of the future, professing "Make America Great Again." Here my focus is not the politics, but the psychological aspects of the slogan.

A simultaneous reference to the past as great and a suggestion that we are no longer great and need to revisit that time is both subtle and brilliant marketing. Our mind softens the past, smoothes out the rough edges, and mutes the negative experiences of life in favor of positive memories. Thus, we naturally hold fond memories of the past—the good old days. Next, danger is like crack cocaine for the primordial part of our brain, the amygdala, which looks for and expects danger at every turn. Priming the amygdala with negative or emotionally charged words puts our brains on high alert, suggesting there are nefarious forces at work. At this point, the caveman brain takes over.

If you are focusing energy on the immediate, the now, and it's an emergency, you don't have any energy left to think of the future. All available energy is diverted to the present; the wagons have become circled. Incidentally that past president didn't come up with the slogan "Make America Great Again," but borrowed, and then copywrote, it from Ronald Reagan in the 1980s, another great marketing move.

What does mental manipulation, using divisive language, weaponizing words, and priming, do to us? For one thing, it can rob us of a future. Second, we no longer give each other second chances, or even second glances. We judge unfairly, become impatient, and forgo reflection in the name of time; we no longer give each other "do-overs" like we did when we were kids. Like the story of the frog in the pot of boiling water, we are slowly taught to be unempathetic and uncaring. These are the effects of the arrogance of ignorance. Once we are trained in this protective impulse path of stimulus/response, the behavior becomes second nature, and we now have less of a problem being Machiavellian to one another and playing a zero-sum game with coworkers, collaborators, and strangers. My success now depends (in large part) on your failure, and everyone is potentially my enemy. There become few safe places.

If it's not our leaders professing the sky is falling, then it's some home security company suggesting there are burglars and thieves looming outside our door, or a software company telling us our identities are being stolen, or the media looking for whatever elicits an emotional response in us and then searching for more of it to keep our focus and keep their ratings high. It reminds me of the

2005 Eagles song, "Dirty Laundry." It's time for us to stop being manipulated, take our brains out of neutral and move them into drive, and reconnect with people at a personal level.

Consider that those who would divide us have a reason for doing so. What is it? If anyone is whispering in your ear that you need to be careful and selfish, watch your neighbor, limit communication, hoard your resources and knowledge, and only listen to them, I hope it sends up flags. I would hope you ask questions.

Cynicism Versus Reaching Out

Retired Marine Corps General and former Secretary of Defense James Mattis recently said in an article, "Cynicism is not only the enemy of consensus building, it's also cowardice." "Cynicism," he said, "fosters a distrust of reality; it provokes suspicion that hidden forces are at play and instills a sense of victimhood and though it may be physically gratifying, solves nothing." He's right!

To shake off this cynicism, we need to think, reflect, and serve others. Being helpful is perhaps the greatest and most rewarding feeling a human being can have. Our responsibility is and should be to one another first. We should start and end every day by being helpful. How else do we move forward? We need to become aware of our motivations and influences and question where they come from. Next, we need to be aware of where we are spending our resources (time, energy, and money). Where our time and money are being influenced to be spent, do the two agree?

The Age of Wisdom

We have gone from an agrarian age to a *science age*, an *industrial age*, a *technological age*, and an *information and knowledge age*. What's next? Welcome to the *age of wisdom*. If we consider the act of "knowing," we can visualize an ascending line from left to right consisting of "data," "information," "knowledge," and finally "wisdom." We are awash with data points which, when put together, make information. String this information together and we manifest usable knowledge we can use to manipulate and influence things in useful ways.

Here's an example. I see a key on my kitchen counter (a data point), and I identify it as an automobile key (another data point) of a specific make (data point). The key is sitting on a piece of paper which has writing on it (more data points), and I recognize the words as grocery store items and the paper as a list and looking out the window I see the automobile (data point, data point, data point). I can now sort these information strings (made of data points) together into usable knowledge that someone, maybe me, will be going to the grocery store. But where does wisdom come in? As I reflect on this knowledge I compiled by collecting details, I now move my focus in the opposite direction, widening my thoughts more broadly, opening the aperture, and reflecting on the best ways to execute this data, information, and knowledge. If I retrieve groceries from the store, I've successfully accomplished my task. But what if I could accomplish more in this act? What if my endeavor not only supported myself in that present experience but also supported myself in the future (I could get groceries for tomorrow as well), as well as supported my family, neighbors, and community. You get the idea. I scale out my thinking after first zooming in and collecting. When I've done these thought calculations, I pick up my key and go. That's an example of practicing wisdom. The brain is a muscle like any other; the more you exercise it, the stronger it will become.

Escaping the Arrogance of Ignorance

The *arrogance of ignorance is* the defensive, intolerant, cynical, and selfish mindset that is threatening to become the epidemic of our time. This way of thinking you're being encouraged to practice is a manipulative sham. It's not flattering to you or your family, and it neither serves nor supports the betterment of humanity. There is no "smash-and-grab" looter scenario playing out here in which the world's few remaining resources are being divvied up and distributed to the most cunning and powerful among us. Don't drink this Kool-Aid.

There is a tomorrow around the corner and it's bright, but to get there we must first make a turbulent transition. Change is always a little sporty, so enjoy the fast ride. Come out of your cave and coax others out. Turn off the TV and turn on to your neighbors. Break ties with your doomsday prepper friends and stop watching *The Walking Dead*. Don't get discouraged, and don't be disheartened.

In this increasingly complex, diverse, more connected world, there are certainly many challenges. Chief among them is building courage, maintaining awareness, suspending judgment, thinking wisely, and supporting inclusion, tolerance, and dialogue. What do things like willful ignorance, cynicism, fear, and malicious manipulation from others do for the unthinking mind? They kill it. Unthinking is fueled by intuition, gives birth to creativity, and is inspired by the promise of a new and better tomorrow. When tomorrow is blocked from our view, unthinking is also blocked, gray matter shrinks, and we only think of now—survival, nothing more.

PART 3:
UNTHINKING OTHERS

Storm in a Teacup:
Understand the Battle, End the War

Maybe you've had the misfortune of having war brought to your doorstep. If so, my empathy and wish for your safety go out to you and your family. But maybe you just feel as if a cloak of conflict is wrapped all around you continually, threatening everything you value and hold dear. What's going on today to make us feel this way?

It certainly feels as if even if we are not caught up in a literal war, we are at a menacing precipice, at the edge of a cliff from which we will surely fall and perish. What's worse is when we search our memory for a time in our life when this has happened before, we can't recall any. If this feels like your world, you're not alone.

But what if the current tempest surrounding you is largely your own doing—or at the least of your own allowing? Even if you can't do something about external conflict, you can do something about internal conflict. Let's look at what's going on today, what can be done about it (personally and professionally), how you can be a compass for others trying to navigate to a tranquil peaceful place, and how to live a contented, meaningful, and secure life at work and at home.

What's Really Going On?

First off, there *is* a war going on today, and it's mostly a war for your attention and control. That's just one piece of this puzzle. There absolutely is a systematic, methodical, and relentless campaign afoot to keep you off track, distracted, hyperfocused in a particular direction, fearful, and physically and mentally exhausted. You're not imagining things.

Why is the world so often like this? Is it simply marketing and advertising? I'll leave those conclusions to you. However, my personal feeling is that it's probably not due to a global organized and clandestine conspiracy bent on destroying us, though some might currently disagree. More likely, we as a species are just too stupid at this juncture in humanity to realize that cheap attempts at manipulation for personal gain and agenda are an unhealthy (and unsustainable) trajectory for humankind to continue to follow. What's worse is that we're also playing off one another's behavior. We have *mirror neurons* in our brain to thank for this. I have a skilled hypnotherapist friend in a nearby town who says they've been seeing an increase of anxiety and stress around the world in recent years, and much of it stems from *amygdala hijack* and triggering.

Another part of what's happening is that we live in perhaps the most stimulating, tumultuous, exciting, diverse, dynamic, and rapidly changing time in human history. While we should feel very fortunate to be alive during such an amazing time, it's no wonder we suffer from things like attention deficit disorder and attention deficit hyperactivity disorder in the 21st century, which, interestingly enough, has now been diagnosed in the elderly.

Finally, for the first time in history, more people have knowledge of the world at their fingertips. We are suddenly paralyzed by the realization that we are awash in data, information, and knowledge about virtually anything we would care and not care to know, and quite frankly it's freaking us out. How do we pull all of this together and find wisdom? With this new ability to know, consider, and integrate concurrent knowledge of the past, present, and a better possible picture of the future, it's like we're getting a taste of what it is to be "omniscient," and it's overwhelming.

Triggers and Hijacking

Amygdala hijack, a term coined by author Daniel Goleman, happens when our brain gets forced into a *fight, flight,* or *freeze* situation caused by the sudden onset of stimulus to the amygdala, the very old (300 million years) emotional/irrational part of the brain. If the amygdala receives stimulus before the neocortex does, the newest thinking /rational part of the brain (3 million years), then the mind reacts (is triggered) in an irrational or destructive way as if it's in a threatening situation. Voila, you've been hijacked. What can trigger us? Just about anything.

The purpose of emotions, Goleman said, is to make us pay attention right now. Emotions help us execute an immediate action plan. These plans are tactical (short term) and not strategic (long term). To potentially make matters worse, hijacking is contagious. If you've ever witnessed your parents break into an argument over being lost or discussing something sensitive like money, then you know what hijacking looks like. Similarly, if an angered dog in an otherwise docile pack were to suddenly bite another, that emotion would instantly spread, exploding into bites all over the place without the other dogs even knowing why they're biting. Interestingly, amygdala hijack can also occur in moments of intense joy, as when someone tells a joke resulting in uproarious laughter.

This is particularly interesting because traditional workplace structures have followed a motivational model centered around invoking fear to exact control from a workforce in order to ensure production. This traditional tool (fear) in managers and leaders' toolboxes may no longer work in the 21st century if they hope to win over hearts and heads in addition to a pair of hands. Laughter and joy are more sustainable, endearing, and *strategic* motivators than fear. Organizational ambidexterity, a new way of doing business involving the balancing of *exploitation* of known learning with *exploration* of new learning and innovation, has dispensed with fear-based motivation models in place of workplace cultures and structures that support strategic force multipliers like encouragement, support, and love.

Reasons for Turmoil

The industrial revolution ended over a century ago; however, the top-down hierarchical structures, strict authoritarian models, and fear-based cultures persist. Not only do they persist but there's evidence to suggest they may be experiencing a revival. Why does it seem like some organizations are doubling down on cracking a whip for old ways of doing business instead of facing an unknown future while others appear to be in perpetual chaos, not knowing what strategies to employ? To answer the first question, it's because it's familiar. We don't know what else to do, and this is hard stuff. Humanity is sailing into uncharted waters and referring to past success models is all we can think of. It's muscle memory mixed with a desperate play for something time tested and familiar that once worked, but probably won't anymore.

Science fiction writer William Gibson said, "The future is here, it's just not evenly distributed." He's right. We are living in an unevenly distributed reality, a diverse mosh-pit of old, current, and new technology, thinking, skills, beliefs, experiences, people, and stories. With it often comes an "anything and everything goes" mentality. At times, we rely on the "tried and true," and at other times we try anything, throwing something at the wall to see what sticks. This can be a great strategy to employ along with "business as usual" so long as we know why and when it works, and we learn from it.

Old and New Models

The models of yesterday won't always work today. New models are needed like Dave Snowden's *Cynefin framework* (pronounced CA-NAV-IN). A sensemaking decision model, it is designed to help make sense of and differentiate between simple, complicated, and complex organizational domains and problems companies face.

Today, many organizational members problem solve from their unique skill sets and preferences. However, the scene quickly becomes disorderly and chaotic if we don't first know the nature of the problem and which approach and experts are needed. This is where Snowden's model is extremely useful. Unlike classic two-by-two grid framework consultancy models, where data are categorized into predefined boxes and then interpreted accordingly, Cynefin works the other way around. In this sensemaking decision model, data precede frameworks; patterns (frameworks) emerge from the data in a social process. Categorization models are very attractive because they're familiar and fast, operating on the assumption that the process (situation) is simple and known (familiar), and therefore best practice can be determined and applied quickly and easily. These models are great for *exploitation* of the known but not *exploration* of the new or novel. In a complicated or complex situation in which there could be thousands of influencing modulators, of which little may be known, best practice should not be applied and could be harmful.

There are also leaders today who hold memories of industrial revolution era practices, either experiencing them firsthand or taught to them by mentors. The challenge of change is perhaps greatest for these people to be open, probe, and allow new thinking and experiences to enter their purview. It's time to share new updated learning and execute better models. It's been said that "the best time to plant a tree was 30 years ago; the second-best time is right now."

Carrots or Sticks?

In her book *The Evolved Executive,* Heather Wickman proposed a radical solution for transformative change in business: love. Before you balk or make judgments of what you might think is an unrealistic or liberal view, let's talk about what Heather means. It's both amazing and potentially game changing.

She's not talking about a motherly type of love that hugs us and protects us from harm. Instead, it's a courageous empathetic love for one another that moves in a way that bestows trust, suspends judgment, promotes openness, and defers decisions until a clear picture emerges. This kind of respectful care allows others the room and freedom to move, express themselves, and act in undeterminable ways, trusting in outcomes and the relevance and significance they will produce. Quelling our fears of chaos from a more relaxed, less controlling stance takes courage and ironically heightened self-control. However, developing these skills and practicing this kind of respect pays big dividends and allows the universe to assemble a picture for us beyond our expectations and imagination.

Heather said we have been operating from old paradigms, using old language, and that fear as a motivator is both "inefficient and toxic." She's right. For one thing, when we are in a state of fear, we will only work to get ourselves out of that state and back to a safe place. Once we are safe, activity will stop, and we go back to conserving our resources in anticipation of another attack. For this reason, this type of motivation only produces short-term results; it's tactical and not strategic in nature. Fear receptors in the brain routinely triggered will lay down familiar pathways the mind revisits, discouraging long-term thinking in favor of survival in the moment. These habitual patterns change the brain, and we learn to be afraid and hunker down. The brain physically shrinks. Finally, considering that mirror neurons cause us to mimic one another's behavior, when this scenario is scaled up from the individual to a team, department, division, or organization, fear is toxic to your climate and your culture.

I have a friend named Jim who has been studying *presenteeism* for years. Jim says presenteeism is 10 times worse than absenteeism. Why? Because absent employees are not present at work during intended leave. If their absence were due to illness or a negative, depressed, or degraded mental state, its observation would adversely affect others. Diminished, anxious, or unhappy workers also affect the mood of those they encounter. As a bit of actionable advice, observe your daily office climate and your organization's culture for a week and tell me what you see. Does it seem open? Does it appear healthy? What do you notice?

Slowing Down and Getting Balance Back

In some ways it feels as if the universe just grabbed the emergency brake on the train and pulled it hard. If this is its way of sending us a message, that message might be to slow down and pay more attention to the balance and interconnectedness among all things. According to Ian McGilchrist in his book *The Master and His Emissary*, humanity is *exploratively* and *exploitatively* out of balance and has been moving more so for centuries, since the Augustan era, in favor of an idealistic "left-brained" world.

As we busily narrow and converge on repetition of the known and familiar, we benefit from increased performance, efficiency, and output of that which we already do well. However, we forfeit how to learn and explore and lose part of what it is to be human in the process. We lose the muscle memory to embrace life's infinite possibilities and recognize its surprising unknown unknowns, potentially throwing away a utopian best future. Recent events have shown us a world capable of rapid change in which nature can suddenly and unapologetically invoke new rules. In light of this, is our resistance to change, repetition of processes for their own sake, and endorsement of the familiar in the name of comfort proving to be a foolish game?

The New Disrupter

In my first book, *The Rise of the Ambidextrous Organization*, I talk about two different kinds of learning companies must engage in to be healthy and sustainable for the long haul, both in work and in the individual lives of their workers. These are *exploitative learning*, refinement of what they already know, and *explorative learning*, completely new and novel learning. One of the biggest challenges humanity faces is a world woefully out of balance regarding learning, with societies driving too much effort and attention toward the exploitative side of life (what is already known) and not enough on the explorative (what is new). Not only do organizations encourage this behavior, they prefer and even demand it for obvious business reasons. Increased monetary profit, increased performance, and increased efficiency are all solid fiscal reasons to keep the foot on the gas pedal and to drive familiar roads. Suddenly, however, this strategy no longer works as we find ourselves in a new place confronted with never-before-seen challenges.

Humanity is being faced with a challenge on a global scale that has no regard for business as usual and one that came upon us, as Hemingway once said, "first gradually, then suddenly." It has been said that with every challenge there is also opportunity, and the novel coronavirus of 2020 is no exception—that is, if we see it as such and act on what we see. It's an opportunity to take stock of how we have done, and done things, so far, not just as leaders, managers, and workers but also as citizens of our communities and as a species. Taking this opportunity for reflection allows us a chance to balance the ledger, because if we choose to, we could make new corrections and begin again on a better course.

The "Conscripted" Ambidexterity of a Pandemic

In the 40 years of research on the subject of organizational ambidexterity—the ability to both "exploit" and "explore" the environment doing what you have learned to do well and simultaneously learn new things—three types have been identified and studied: *temporal, structural,* and *contextual ambidexterity.* I propose a fourth type has emerged, a trigger perturbing our cherished exploitative processes and one that is not intentional, expected, or welcome. This is a "conscripted" or "forced" kind of ambidexterity, one that was "unintended" and with mandatory enrollment. The novel coronavirus (COVID-19) pandemic which appeared first in December of 2019 is quickly changing the face of humanity and business, forcing organizations and governments to rethink, rearrange, and reinvent their processes for operating in a new environment. If one thing is certain, it's that this is a potentially "ambidextrous" triggering event for humanity. While opting out of change in the face of such an event might be possible, it would also likely be fatal.

Conscripted ambidexterity is defined as

- Having a "punctuated," "revolutionary" onset (vs evolutionary over time)
- Being irreconcilable under current behaviors, models, and paradigms
- Having a conscripting nature (mandatory enrollment)
- Deriving from the natural world
- Emerging without human intention
- Requiring agency (action)

Humanity's progression up to now has been wonderful for many, but troublesome for others, unviable and untenable. The relentless demand for efficiency, the disenfranchisement and neglect of those we deem valueless, and the growing salary gap despite decades of productivity and progress increases are suddenly coming to light. Let's look at some of these good and bad results of this event.

Our Treatment of the Elderly, Young, and Those Considered Less Valuable

About 1.3 million people live in the nation's 15,600 nursing homes according to the Centers for Disease Control and Prevention. Most nursing homes have had problems managing infections even when there's not a pandemic. Most of our country's nursing care facilities are inadequately staffed or poorly managed. According to *USA Today*, at least 2,300 long-term care facilities in 37 states have reported positive cases of COVID-19 and more than 3,000 residents have died since December 2019. These numbers are thought to be underestimated, as there are not enough tests for the residents.

Lack of Empathy, Responsibility, and Connection

Some people, even public officials, show little empathy for others. In U.S. prisons, there were 9,400 COVID cases at the onset of the pandemic and officials weren't responding quickly or doing enough. Critics have indicated that a lack of personal protective equipment (PPE) and inadequate testing caused a public health disaster.

A battle also erupted that could have been as significant as the days of Jimmy Hoffa and the teamsters, and for good reason. Tyson Foods set the stage for it by demanding, with the help of the federal government, that workers come back to work in meat processing plants at the height of the pandemic despite deplorably unsafe working conditions. The president addressed the issue of possible meat shortages by signing an executive order that said meat processing plants are part of the nation's critical infrastructure and must remain open to ensure a "continued supply of protein for Americans." This is despite the fact that 90% of the 1,326 people testing positive for COVID-19 in Black Hawk County, Iowa, were tied to the Tyson pork processing plant. Incidentally, protein also comes from plants; that's what cattle eat.

A Dwindling Middle Class

In *Winners Take All*, Anand Giridharadas said middle-class worker salaries have not risen significantly—with less than a 10%

median wage increases since 1972—despite the fact that worker productivity has increased by over than 70%. Where has all this profit been going? Increasing pay inequalities are leading to a dwindling middle class, and the gap between the richest and poorest families is the widest it has been in 50 years.

Global Elites, Corporate Billionaires, and Leaders

Billionaires have a responsibility to share the success you have helped them achieve. Global elites would like you to think they are just like you, that they empathize with your plight and have the same struggles you do. According to Giridharadas, however, they play a charade, only pretending to care. Jeff Bezos recently took heat for not taking care of his workers' safety in the Amazon fulfillment centers, and it's been reported that other large companies have been woefully late in providing masks for employees and creating safer working conditions. Many quarantined Americans are arbitrarily not being allowed to telework and are simply being laid off without pay instead of dipping into company capital and profits to care for them.

At the time of writing this, over 30 million Americans had filed for jobless aid in the 6 weeks since the COVID outbreak began. Speaking of global elites and corporate billionaires marketing themselves as being like the struggling common man, an altered version of the "Keep on trucking" slogan was recently used by a global corporate billionaire for an upcoming reelection campaign. The original came from a popular 1970s anti-establishment counter-culture drug movement started in California.

True Intent

Ignorance comes in two forms, *willful stupidity* and *not knowing*. The type you favor speaks to your intent. I watched the classic 1982 sci-fi film *Blade Runner* the other day, and in it the main character Harrison Ford jumps into a flying car for a trip across Los Angeles. The film is set in 2019. Where are the flying cars and other automated stuff we were promised decades ago? I still remember *The Jetsons* and wanting a Rosie the robot maid and conveyer belts in my house. Why don't we have these things? One logical reason is that we have not progressed as we could because companies and leaders are comfortable and profitable in their current *exploitative* paradigms. Puncture-less tires vs. inflatable rubber tires, electric and hydrogen cars vs. combustion engine vehicles, safer nuclear power vs. coal, plant-based proteins vs. meat-based proteins are all examples of technologies that have persisted and dominated because someone is currently profiting from them. I'm ready for my flying car.

Telework

Telework has been around a long time, but we have yet to perfect it or trust our people to use it wisely and productively. It's time to try. Are you a "Theory X" or "Theory Y" manager? Theory X holds that, left to their own devices, workers will lie, cheat, and steal, while Theory Y holds that workers are conscientious and inherently want to be productive and do the right thing. It's difficult to get an accounting regarding what workers would do if left to their own devices, and this makes leaders and managers nervous. We need to try and trust them to do the right thing because to not do so would send a troubling message of distrust, which would wreak havoc on an organization's climate and culture.

Positive Results of the Pandemic

Pollution and Carbon Decrease

Our world is a little cleaner as a result of less pollutants being put into our atmosphere and our water. People are driving less, boating less, and polluting less. Canals in Venice are cleaner than they have been in years, and so are the skies over Los Angeles.

Commutes

My 10-mile commute to work each day used to take me 45 minutes to an hour of stop-and-go driving, and sometimes the ride home took an hour and a half. I never realized it before, but I would often arrive to work triggered and wound up, grumbling and ready to snap at the first person who looked at me cross-eyed. Now my commute is a breezy 15 to 20 minutes of nonstop driving and there's no congestion in the office because we are working alternate shifts, with employees teleworking every other day. No one is on top of anyone anymore or intruding in their spaces, on the road, or in the office.

Distancing, Responsibility, and Respect

People are more respectful and thoughtful of one another and each other's personal space, and they're also more responsible with common areas. It's disgusting to say, but I used to witness people not washing their hands regularly in restrooms. Not anymore. Transportation, theaters, cruise ships, and airlines are rethinking their business models, because I don't think people will stand for being packed into boats and planes anymore. I remember just a year or two ago hearing about an airline that had submitted a patent for reclined hammock style seating so they could get a few more rows in planes. You would basically be standing up while leaning backwards. No thanks.

Slowing Down

This pandemic has cobbled us, and that's good. Life has slowed down and become more thoughtful and deliberate. Teleworking several days a week means I'm driving less and being more deliberate when I do drive. No more daily runs to the convenience store for one item. If I need things from the store, I'll get them on a day I also go into the office. I'm more comfortable, happier, and find myself more efficient and productive with this new normal, but there are many who are not. Their minds and bodies are restless, and they crave distraction. Buddhists call this "monkey mind." Perhaps mindfulness discipline training combined with a slower pace would help them cull their anxiety, find peace and calm, and be more productive and happy.

Making the Next Move

In response to the pandemic or other big life disruptors, what can you do? You can modify your behavior and act on your better nature for one thing. My daughter and I recently had a conversation about her driving into a neighboring state to spend the weekend with her boyfriend. Our state did not allow interstate travel without good reason, such as work or health. While she understood the reasons, she was conflicted. She had a friend who was skirting the rules daily for similar reasons with a defunct letter for a job they no longer had, and we have family friends who frequently cross state lines to visit a second home. While these people relaxed the rules in those instances, they're not bad or unethical; on the contrary, they're great people. But if something were to have happened, they would have had to live with that burden. My daughter has had to reconcile their decisions by questioning her own, making thoughtful choices.

Though some remain aloof and indifferent to change, with their heels dug in or protesting for a pre-COVID-19 world, public dialogue questioning the status quo and promoting change is encouraging. Along with this pandemic have come questions, and encouragingly I've heard my leadership asking questions in public forums that I have been asking privately: How should we behave now? What are we doing differently that's better? What moves should we make next and in the future? This crisis, thrust upon us all, has brought us to an interesting crossroads. The way we turn will make all the difference.

What's wrong with our past strategies? The problem we face now is exacerbated by the very strategy we've executed up to now. The problem with our strategy is that it has spent too much time on one side of an ambidexterity equation, the exploitative side. It hasn't been an ambidextrous model at all. Focusing too much time and effort on exploitation, cutting out everyone and everything that doesn't fit with its traditional model of executing today's activities in the same old ways, often feels productive and efficient—but it's not, and it won't get all of us out of this crisis.

Up to now, we have often disenfranchised and marginalized the most explorative and creative among us for purely lazy, selfish, or fearful reasons. We've cut off the ends of our bell curves to refine the mean. When we exclusively engage in yesterday's familiar work, we define a narrow bandwidth for value and disregard or marginalize virtually everyone different who didn't make the cut—our very young and very old, women, our gritty and courageous learners and mistake makers, our slow thinkers, and slow learners, and those thought to be cognitively or physically disabled and deficient. A scary problem with this is when we're suddenly faced with a world which is nothing like yesterday, we become stuck. Not only do we become stuck but we're also likely to make fatal decisions because we're frantically bailing out a boat with a homogeneous, like-minded crew. In other words, we have likely long ago silenced and kicked everyone off the bus who could have offered the question that provides the breakthrough answer we needed. With our scramble to establish a new normal, we are being forced to answer to our past value sets. We must decide what stays and what goes. To our chagrin, in the process of this balancing of the ledger, we are being shown what our true nature has been.

See You on the Other Side!

I predicted at the time of writing this that sometime in the near future we would all get together again, perhaps for dinner or a drink, and it has come to pass. It happened when a vaccine was created, when we built adequate antibodies, and when the world was a healthier place. This phenomenon not only forced our hand regarding the necessity of our cherished routines, but it also exposed unhealed societal wounds long hidden under Band-Aids, and it shone a light in dark corners where we'd rather not have looked in the past. It's all being churned up like so many shipwrecks from storms past.

The problems and challenges we now face are problems ambidextrous organizations have learned to turn into growth and fortune. This phenomenon, this pandemic, was a major learning disrupter for humankind, similar to the kinds I research and write about. Ambidextrous organizations routinely leverage challenge for genuine breakthrough success in the business world. For them, such challenges are their four-leaf clovers, in (for them) what are a cultivated field of four-leaf clovers. Though this challenge is different from ambidextrous organizations' business challenges of the past for obvious reasons—it's global, it deals with life and not just business, and it's life threatening—it still presented a learning challenge and opportunity for growth. How do we as a new emerging global society create better processes and rules that benefit everyone? How do we fix our assisted living facilities, behave inclusively, reduce our carbon footprint, slow down our acquisitive impulses, relax, learn empathy, raise our impoverished, bring back the middle class, hold our elites and leaders accountable, honor a triple bottom line, and get more cars off the road and create new green spaces? I can't answer those questions specifically, but I can ask them and so can you, and we can all think about and discuss them together. What has this global disrupter done for the practice of unthinking? Unlike the effects discussed in the last chapter, of fear, pessimism, cynicism, and defensiveness and its constricting effect, it's awakened and revitalized unthinking. If you tune your perception and observation and look around, you will notice that the pandemic of 2020 has taken the box of puzzle pieces and shaken them up, revealing a brand-new picture.

PART 4:
CREATING AN UNTHINKING YOU

Harnessing the Power of Storytelling for Good

Tell me a story. What came to mind when I made that request? A personal experience, something you recently read, an anecdote a friend shared, or a movie remembered from childhood? Whatever the case, chances are it activated more parts of your brain than other types of inquiry, invoking more thought and feeling. The interesting thing about stories is that they're everywhere. They are the tapestry that covers life and, in a moment, can transport us to other worlds and frames of mind, inspiring, captivating, or affirming.

But stories today are not what they used to be. They've changed from what they once were, in their use, in their telling, and in our perception of them. We are less likely to trust stories we hear, when we are even aware we're being told one. There are lots of reasons for this, some good, some not, and some perhaps we can chalk up to evolution. This chapter takes a closer look at storytelling in the modern era, putting you on a path to a better you and a better world. What's the connection between storytelling and unthinking? Think of storytelling as the medium the unthinking subconscious intuition uses to imagine, examine, and make sense of reality's landscape and best inform the conscious mind.

Storytelling Today

There are a lot of stories out there today, and unfortunately many of them are bad—bad for our health, mental and physical, and being told for bad reasons. That's the bad news. Designed to ensnare, control, manipulate, frighten, confuse, or escape any functional reality, the worst ones are mostly stitched-together cautionary tales and horror stories meant to trigger the amygdala and keep us in line or in retreat and producing cortisol. When we do hear a good story, one with moral or ethical principles, or one that gives us hope, insight, or power and energy, we either overlook it or quickly pocket it as were undoubtedly anticipating the next menacing story, which feels as regular as passing busses on a city street. One of the most powerful aspects of stories is their ubiquity, and the other is their reach. They're everywhere and they permeate deep into us. The good news is that the same powerful qualities that have allowed humanity to weaponize stories against each other can also be used to free us from worry—and the great news is now you know this. Listen for and question the subtle stories you pick up on from others. Do they serve you?

Where have all the virtuous stories gone? Stories have been largely hijacked today and are used for all manner of nefarious or unfortunate reasons. Conspiracy theories might be the worst. Not too long ago, I got taken in by a conspiracy theory video I watched in a social media post and as a result walked around in a funk for the better part of a day, suspicious, discouraged, and convinced that organizations and humanity in general couldn't be trusted. Once I realized I'd been deceived, and the video was nothing more than a very well-made compilation of unrelated (and bad) events, I had to laugh at myself. My brain had taken me by the hand and spirited me down a frightening and very real feeling path without my realizing.

Companies can feel like this sometimes too, like callous, corrupt, manipulative, or toxic places that hum along with syncopated psychosis and malice. Storytelling author Donald Miller said the reason we can at times be deceived by things like this is because the mind is hardwired to see patterns. It rejects randomness in place of linking things together; it can't help it. As a great VOX article by Brian Resnick proves, the mind is the biggest storyteller of all, constructing a reality rooted in previous life experience from familiar filtering schemes and bending our perception of reality to meet our desires and expectations. So the next time one of your very smart coworkers says they have the company figured out in one big, connected maniacal conspiracy theory, think about actor Russell Crowe in the movie *A Beautiful Mind* and take what they say with a large dose of skepticism and thought.

In my research on storytelling, I read everything current I could find on the subject. What follows is a compilation of notes from books and articles on storytelling.

Neuroscience

Shane Snow said that stories create empathy. When a story is told, more parts of the brain become activated than when mere data is transmitted. Stories activate emotional centers of the brain as well as rational logic centers and creative artistic centers. As the saying goes, "Neurons that fire together, wire together," so the more parts of your brain that get stimulated during an experience, the more probable it is you will learn and remember it and think, or *unthink*, in new ways. Writer and storyteller Gabrielle Dolan explained that unlike data, stories stimulate the neocortex of the brain and generate oxytocin, the chemical known as "the love drug," garnering safety, security, and trust. Navigating the world using storytelling as one of the tools provides deeper context, greater insight, and richer understanding, engaging both the conscious and subconscious mind.

In the great book *Moonwalking with Einstein*, Joshua Foer revealed a secret known by the ancient Greeks regarding memory and the brain called the *memory palace*. Before the 5th century BC, everything was committed to memory and the greatest compliment that could be bestowed on a person was to say that he or she had a superior memory. There were Greek orators and statesmen who knew the names of every soldier in the Roman army and could recite plays and speeches completely from memory. How did they do it? They understood two important facts about how the brain works. The first is that our minds remember routes through space. If you were to close your eyes right now and picture yourself walking through your house or driving to work, you could do it with vivid detail. The second is that the brain is very good at remembering anything shocking, salacious, exciting, or frightening. Put those two memory tricks together and you have a memory palace, a story you can recall in your head to remember anything. Besides making a memory palace from the layout of my house and then using it to remember grocery items on a list (imagine yourself walking through your house retrieving those items placed in different rooms), I have also made memory palaces of celebrities, automobile collections, and favorite memorable movies.

Evolution

Ekaterina Walter said that, evolutionarily speaking, we as a species have dealt with imagery far longer than we have dealt with language and the written word. For this reason, the brain processes imagery faster than it does words. Author Paul Smith explained that when we receive information through a story, we receive a more comprehensive picture and, when facts are woven into stories, we are 20 times more likely to remember them.

Learning

Smith went on to say that unlike data or facts, a story reaches every type of learner. Forty percent of us are visual learners, 40% of us are auditory learners, and 20% are kinetic learners. The imagery in a story speaks to the visual learner; vocabulary, tone, and inflection reach the auditory learner; and emotions and feelings connect with the kinetic learner.

Author Jonathan Gotschall indicated that stories are often centered around a character in trouble, struggling, or faced with a challenge; as a result, they help us practice and resolve real-life problems. Author Will Storr agreed, stating that one of the chief reasons we're so interested in flawed characters is because they create a safe space for us to explore our own flaws and what we might do in a similar situation. Interestingly, stories might be the best way transformative change can take hold and new learning can get through to us as our minds and egos work overtime to protect us from our own shortcomings, perceived harm, and change.

Delivery and Execution

I used to think I was a good storyteller, but I discovered I was wrong. I wasn't telling stories. The self-aggrandizing yarns I usually spun to impress my friends were merely anecdotes. Why? Because they didn't contain change. There are certain marks one must hit and elements that must be included for something to count as a story. When I regaled listeners with my anecdotes, it was to gain attention, to impress others, or to get laughs. I'm ashamed to say there was no moral or higher purpose to my stories, just conspicuous attention seeking and empty calories.

For Western stories, Matthew Dicks, author of *Storyworthy*, said that there's traditionally an arc, with a beginning, middle, and end. The crest of the arc represents a significant change in the story, a transformative *5-second moment*. To find the beginning of a story, look to the end; your beginning is usually the opposite of your 5-second moment.

Collective Shiftiness

My friends joke with me all the time that the current craziness in the world is just preparation for the next *bigger* thing. It is acclimating us for the main event, so we won't be too shocked by it. What that event will be, my friends don't say for certain, but they've narrowed it down to either visits from interstellar aliens who make first contact with humanity or the earth cracking open, with pitchfork-wielding devils emerging from the great chasm of fire and smoke to claim dominion over the Earth. Either way, let's get on with it because I'm ready for the fear-mongering to settle down.

Crazy as it might sound, we could probably create a version of either of these shocking realities if we were to buy into such stories long enough, giving them energy. Everything real in our world once began as a thought. Those who would use stories to control and manipulate us know this all too well and use that knowledge to their advantage. Let's look at the disrupters and change brokers currently using stories and the troublesome worlds they often create.

Political Leaders, Governments, and Corporations

If our political leaders, governments, or major corporations tell us a story today, it's likely we will take it with a grain of salt. If we don't, then perhaps we should. Whether it's the promise of a corporation to honor a triple bottom line model of *people, profit,* and *planet* or a government promising fiscal responsibility, it's spurious at best. Case in point, there's so much "spin" in politics, especially during an election year, that I can almost guarantee you that if a political leader is telling you a story it's to influence you toward a specific purpose or agenda you may not be completely aware of. More and more, these leaders are using cognitive bias and mental "sleight-of-hand" tricks to attain those purposes.

Several years ago, a political figure campaigned on a platform referencing a bygone era as preferable to the world we live in today (something virtually unheard of, as most candidates stump on a platform looking forward in time to a better tomorrow). This strategy proved to be troubling, extremely deceiving, and brilliant. By promising constituents a better future by going back to the past, the candidate effectively evoked memories of a bygone era, and those memories were individually different and cognitively flawed and softened.

Neuroscience has proven that as we move away from events, committing them to the past as memories, the rough edges, struggles, pain, and suffering of those experiences fade. What we are left with are the good feelings of that time and memories of the nostalgic "good old days." What's more is that the good old days weren't so good for many ethnicities and demographics. Comparatively, the 1950s and 60s, for example, weren't great for Black Americans (comparatively today they still aren't) or women (comparatively today they still aren't). Cognitively, this is a deceptive technique, as it tricks our brain, and it's despicable if intended. When a leader gives his constituents a promise like making things "great again," never defining, discussing, or asking what that phrase means, it leaves the mind to make predictive assumptions which are likely different than the authors' and produces widely differing opinions.

Media, Marketing, and Advertising

We're aware of the ways in which marketing and advertising use stories to influence. What you may not be aware of, however, is how these stories get in our psyche, influencing and altering our own story, leaving us with unproductive or unhealthy feelings. Our story, once harmonious, can suddenly feel empty and lacking. If it does, you've just been hijacked.

In some countries in the world, however, people still carefully consider the stories they're being told and whether they want to integrate them into their lives. As discussed in Part 2, when a London ad campaign depicted a beautiful tan woman in a bathing suit with the slogan, "Are you beach body ready," there was great public criticism across Europe. Ironically, if this ad appeared in the United States, it's unlikely there would have been any public outcry. Americans would have simply absorbed and internalized the message.

Digitization and Reality

In *Present Shock,* Douglas Rushkoff weaves a story that could ruin traditional storytelling—or could it? In 1970 futurist Alvin Toffler predicted that someday we would reach a state of progress in the world that moved so fast and was so disruptive that humanity would enter an era he called *future shock.* Is it here now? What Rushkoff is referring to is the digital era, a time in history in which everything is happening now, at once. Natural rhythms learned over centuries are being challenged and disrupted, affecting culture, our personal lives, and even our perception of time. One of these disrupted rhythms is stories, and Rushkoff said we now prefer fragmented stories instead of linear ones, adding grievously to our disorientation, as stories are instruments of thought.

Story fragmentation is encouraged by the digital world as it is promoted by everything from flipping through television channels to creating multiple online personas on the internet and social media. We no longer must stay on a continual narrative anymore and are encouraged to be in more than one place at a time. According to Rushkoff, people also conceived of time differently in the predigital era. They considered time to be more linear and thought they could only be in one physical space at a time, and it was where their body happened to be. A predigital person's day would play out like a series of linear stories, and each story would have a specific setting. When you were in a story you were absorbed in it and not connected to other simultaneously unfolding stories. By contrast, in the modern world, people can have a collection of digital selves that take place in other spaces. Though they are no longer physical, each has a story playing out.

94

The immediacy of multiple stories playing out at once also disrupts what the author called the natural "time scales" of things. Our understanding of time scales is now severely muddled, Rushkoff said, and we get confused about things that should operate on slower time scales, like governance for example, which operates in years and decades, vs things which naturally happen on faster scales, like changing fashion trends (seasonally) or political polls (daily). The confusing, distracting, and demanding immediacy of digitization makes us think there is only one time scale, right now.

We are composed of the stories we choose, consciously and unconsciously. As permeable creatures, we absorb them. We breathe in the world around us and with its stories, and we breathe out our new altered stories, and so do organizations. Understanding, living out, and retelling these stories is relatively easy to do with focus, but the digital world is challenging that.

Reality

Digitization aside, until now, scientists have suggested that we live simultaneously on two planes of existence: the observable physical world and the world inside our heads. The reality of life experienced by most is a reconciliation of these two worlds. We have experiences, compare them with our thoughts, and derive a summation of experience at the intersection of the mind and the physical world. We might even live on three planes of existence, the third being a spiritual plane explained by theorists who attest that we are not "physical beings who occasionally have spiritual experiences," but instead are "spiritual beings having a constant physical experience." This physical experience we're immersed in is so pervasive and "in-your-face" with its *visual, auditory, olfactory, tactile,* and *kinetic* sensations, they argue, that we rarely get the chance to see beyond the physical realm and glimpse our spiritual selves. After all, do you think a fish knows that it lives in water and there are other planes of existence out there? Probably not.

But what does all this have to do with your story (or stories)? First, we internalize and absorb stories around us; we have limited control over that. Next, we ourselves are made up of multiple stories (the reality in our heads and the physical world, for example). And last, with the advent of digitization, we can simultaneously live out even more stories, taking on the nonphysical personas of digital identities.

Old Friends

Storytelling works best when it brings diverse groups of strangers together, creates a stronger bond between acquaintances and friends, shares implicit meaning, and garners acceptance, understanding, and trust in a group. I'm working with a group of courageous friends who are repatriating storytelling from the "lions" of government and politics, the "tigers" of media, marketing, and advertising, and the "bears" of digitization and technology, and they're doing it in a way that puts storytelling back in the hands of those who it should belong to—the people living the stories. This international effort made up of master storytellers and researchers from Denmark, the United States, and England is striking new ground and blazing new trails into the uncharted waters of storytelling, story understanding, re-storying, and transformation.

How are they doing it? It begins with awareness and noticing. The True Storytelling Institute has created a storytelling certification program teaching the seven principles of storytelling, which is part mindfulness, part storytelling mechanics, part deep learning, and part coaching and mentoring. The true storytelling course is also about living your best ethical life while making a deeper connection with others and the world around you.

Why should *true* storytelling include ethics? For one thing, pursuing ethics and striving for an ethical life might be the truest expression of fulfillment and freedom. When we establish ourselves ethically and operate from a base of moral principles and ethics, consisting of respected rules of conduct, we free ourselves and others from worry, from burden, from assumption, and from fear. Furthermore, we show others respect and what they will get in a relationship with us from their very first meeting. It's likely you've met people like this before but weren't sure why they were attractive to you. You may have just felt there was something captivating and comforting about them. When you learn to live a life grounded in ethical *true* storytelling, you balance the ledger at the end of every day. You live life and conduct business on a "pay as you go" system and you are neither indebted to anyone in a diminishing way nor owed anything. Your story is both an ongoing one and begins and ends every day. And every day's effort is a personal best as it is no longer compared with yesterday's best.

Living a storytelling life will also help you better organize your life as well as the lives of others. Let's be honest for a moment about people. The insides of some people's heads are like the inside of a haunted house, full of locked rooms, dimly lit spaces, and cobwebs. While this can be entertaining if you are watching it on television, it's unsettling if you're living it. True storytelling will help you open the curtains and bring in the light, sweep the hallways, beat out the rugs, and trim the grounds. Contact my friends Jens, Lena, David, and Grace Ann at True Storytelling Inc. and lift the veil on the clockwork of human interaction, organization, and maybe even the universe using storytelling.

The Storytelling–Ambidexterity, Unthinking Connection

If you've followed my monthly LinkedIn articles, you know my passion and expertise is in the subject of ambidexterity, the balancing of learning strategies in organizations. For organizations that successfully exploit the marketplace doing what they do best for profit, and explore it, learning new things, arriving at ambidexterity is like reaching the emerald city: you're *out of the woods*.

Achieving an ambidextrous organization (or life) is a difficult thing to do, as it's antithetical; it represents balancing contrasting opposites. Usually exploitation of today's known business with today's known practices wins out and organizations and people stop exploring and looking for new things and new ways to do them; they start winding down. You can think of the three types of ambidexterity, temporal, structural, and contextual, like ascending steps, with the first being switching rules (temporal) in which you switch back and forth between exploiting and exploring. The second (structural) is to have a structurally separate space in which to be explorative and creative, and the third one (contextual) gets in your company's DNA, where people are empowered to autonomously pursue the best course of action on any given day (exploit or explore).

Where does storytelling fit in with our different types of ambidexterity? It's fair to say that all organizations practice temporal ambidexterity (switching rules), the first kind. This could be as mundane as Friday afternoon meet-ups at the bar or the company off-site you do once a year at a nature retreat. Some organizations practice structural ambidexterity. Think of aircraft manufacturer Lockheed Martin and its "skunk works" division, which works on discovering and refining tomorrow's aircraft. But few organizations reach the contextual level, and this largely is due to cultural and structural shortcomings (inertia) in the company that won't allow this kind of breakthrough empowerment for their workforce; it's just a bridge too far. Storytelling, however, can build that bridge because it targets culture and breaks up cultural inertia, the tendency for organizations to become too rigid from traditionally held stories, norms, values, and beliefs.

Not only can storytelling change the paralyzing "that's just the way we do things around here" language which cultural inertia brings, it also recalibrates and changes the culture foundationally by promoting psychological safety and a focused attention to detail at the human (personal story) level. When storytelling becomes an organization's currency-changing culture, it then begins to influence and rejig the organization's structure, breaking structural inertia, the tendency for organizations to become too rigid and unable to change their structures and processes. Storytelling is the perfect tool and complement for an ambidextrous organization that has made the paradigm jump from the 20th century business language of Newtonian physics to that of quantum physics. And storytelling organically incorporates the qualities that foster the power of the intuitive, subconscious mind.

Storytelling and the Self-Organizing System

We as humans follow the universe's rule of self-organization and in doing so create the world we walk through every day. Our minds are creation machines, and we are self-organizing systems. As neuroscientist Rudy Tanzi put it, we are a "construct of conscientiousness," a "universe of consciousness." But just because we follow self-organizing laws doesn't mean we have control over any of it. Tanzi said the only role of the mind is to *create*, and that which we create ultimately comes back to govern, regulate, and monitor us. This is where humanity most often goes awry, in trying to control everything.

Tanzi said we can *choose* what we create; our *intention* is the extent of our control, and this in turn dictates our *attention*. This is perhaps the most profound statement I've ever heard regarding living. What do you "choose" to comprise your universe?

Surfing the Day

Planning, preparation, execution, and learning culminate in catching the perfect wave on a day spent surfing. It's the same at the office or at home. Working on a project with colleagues can also be like that day and contain the same elements. Imagine for a moment the activities you might engage in during a day catching waves. Checking weather, driving to the beach before dawn, studying the "break" of the waves, donning your wetsuit, stretching, waxing your board, paddling out, communing with colleagues, smelling the salt air, spotting the right wave, paddling, and getting up on the board, catching the wave. Experience is set by the story you weave into it and make of it. What are the components that make up your workday, your everyday, and what do you bring to it?

Success and Your Story

When I was a kid and even into adulthood, I've thought of myself as a good storyteller and have always been captivated by stories. I hang on them and remember them easily. I haven't always been proud of that, however. When I was younger, I was sometimes looked down upon for telling stories. Scoffed, marginalized, or made fun of, I frequently felt foolish after investing time in stories. Chief dissenters of my adult storytelling seemed to say it was undisciplined (suggesting I lacked discipline), frivolously unserious, or time wasting, but perhaps those people were wrong.

Recently, I shared a story about a military "going away" plaque from the early 1990s I found in storage. As is customary in military units, members are given signed going away pictures when leaving. In the beginning of my military career, I was an apprentice and low in experience and technical ability. As a result, I felt self-conscious and inept, and storytelling didn't help my status with superiors. Perhaps sharing stories was comforting, so I persisted. Though my superior's words rang true, they had little to do with my technical job of fixing aircraft, and for that reason they did feel frivolous.

When I recently found the plaque, I shared it with colleagues because I remembered someone signing it with a comment about storytelling. When searching the messages looking for the one about storytelling, I was astonished by what I found. Instead of there being one note about storytelling on the plaque, virtually every colleague made mention of "Eric the storyteller." Additionally, many thanked me for providing inspiration and motivation using stories.

During a period in my life when I felt powerless, valueless, and ashamed, how could I have not only forgotten but also *missed* my most important contribution to my unit 30 years prior? As it turned out, I did have power and contributed value to my organization and didn't realize it. There's a lesson to be learned from this story, particularly for leaders. All the messages on the plaque were from coworkers and in one case a manager. No one in leadership considered me a motivator or integrator of people; I was regularly appraised (marginally) for technical ability. Moreover, no one could have conveyed these skills to leadership. They were looking for, and telling, a different story they considered more important and valuable.

Storytelling and Truth

There's a saying that "truth doesn't speak to power." As a result, leaders have a hard time finding out what's really going on in their organizations, getting to the truth, and encouraging a safe learning environment. Storytelling, however, is a way to impart valuable truth and instill safety in situations where others might be fearful. Leading with a story motif is a way to provide a safe space to explore with impunity and to collaboratively consider possibilities. I watched my leader do just that recently, deftly framing storytelling to create a safe environment for a busy fragmented department to explore solutions, and it appeared to have worked beautifully.

How can leaders use stories and storytelling to help their teams get "unstuck"? Sometimes a mere suggestion is all it takes. One Tuesday last fall was the beginning of an average week in the office, and we were holding our weekly "roll-up" meeting. Each week a different department briefs their program, outlining their projects, activities, and struggles for other departments. This week, the department noted the four or five things they were currently working on, each one independent and complex, representing significant resource investments. As the brief reached a conclusion, our program manager (the big boss) walked into the conference room unexpectedly after previously dialing into the meeting from his office down the hall. He picked up a marker and began to write on a white board along one wall. He listed the projects briefed in a row and said he wanted to share his thoughts, saying a few words about each.

When he was done, he looked at the team on the video monitor and around the room and said, "I feel like there's a story here about how each of these is connected and how they can support one another. What is that story?" He put the pen down and left the conference room and the meeting continued. Several days later on a conference phone call, the host was reviewing our company's biggest projects and deadlines for a team of engineers when he came to the department that had briefed at the roll-up a few days earlier. Enthusiastically, he told the group, "This one's a good news story. They've figured everything out and will be presenting an overall project plan on Monday." When asked by an attendee how they had worked through their challenges, the engineer leading the meeting said, "I'm not sure. Something happened at another meeting this week and it all just came together!" What happened? Our boss's simple story that day activated and mobilized the group's intuitive, unthinking subconscious minds and the solutions became clear.

From Snakes and Ladders to a Storyboard for Life

During a True Storytelling Conference a few years ago, I helped friends pilot the program's certification process and we were given a homework assignment to "build a storyboard." On it, we were asked to reflect upon our journey and the transformations and changes our lives were making as we helped our story along. As explained by Lena Bruun Jensen, one of the program's founders, we were to "tell us about your life as you begin staging the launch of your new story."

After thinking about it for a while, I intuitively went to a secondhand thrift store. Partly out of laziness and not wanting to re-invent the wheel and partly drawn there because of a childhood memory, I found exactly what I was looking for. It was a game called *Chutes and Ladders*, mass produced by the Milton Bradley company in 1943. The game dates back to ancient India and was first called Moksha Patam (Snakes and Ladders). Originally about morality lessons, the game was used to teach the young about virtues (ladders) and vices (snakes). In the original version of the game, there were more snakes than ladders to depict more evil in the world than virtue. In the center of the board there's one long ladder and one long chute. As it turned out, it was the perfect backdrop to illustrate my journey. Going forward, I will forever filter my life's journey through the snakes and ladders lens.

In my storyboard, shown below, there are brick walls and governors. The first brick wall depicted is at the top of the first ladder. In the traditional game, you move across the board from left to right and from bottom to top after the roll of dice. As a modified gameboard/ storyboard, my board is meant to be interpreted as either my daily journey or life journey dependent upon what story is being told. In the lower left corner of the board (square 1), there is immediately a ladder, and there are written the words *contribution, effort, gift.* The idea here is that we set out each day with the desire (and opportunity) to make a contribution, put forth an effort to be helpful, or bring a gift to the universe, and this desire and effort gives us an opportunity to climb a ladder and (in this case) move some 36 spaces in ascent on the board. On my storyboard, this ascension represents and symbolizes an opportunity to "move up" in my life in levels of understanding, clarity, and contentment.

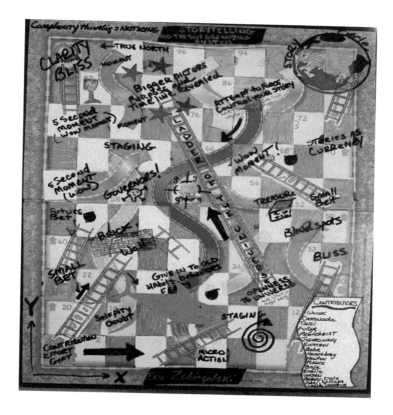

But our efforts and what we bring to life may not meet our expectations and be received as we had hoped. Our contributions may not be appreciated, understood, needed, or considered of value; we may hit a brick wall. As the saying goes, "Life is not what happens to us but how we react to it." What we do next is key in our story. Do we slide down a chute in despair, self-pity, and doubt, abandon our efforts and contribution never to revisit them again, or do we mindfully observe unexpected responses and wait to see if the universe has some other path or purpose in mind?

Governors are something I have written about before. Like brick walls, they can impede us, but unlike them, they don't stop us dead in our tracks. Sometimes imposed by others and sometimes by us, they regulate our progress and set borders and boundaries. The thing about governors in our life is this: like the tale of *Icarus*, there is danger in flying both too high and close to the sun (and melting our wings) and too low and close to the sea (and weighing them down). We must periodically take account and question the governors regulating us: Do we need them? Are they helping or hurting us? Do we have the complete story and picture? Curiously, when we hear the story of Icarus we usually hear the part of flying too high but not of flying too low.

Five-Second Moments, Small Bets, and Micro Actions

Every Western story has a beginning, middle, and end. Somewhere around the middle (the arc of the story), our hero is faced with a dilemma, a revelation, or a challenge—often a situation opposite that when the story began. Maybe it even surprises them. This "wow" moment is in stark contrast to where you previously were. That's the 5-second moment.

In contrast to the brick wall that stops you and shuts you down, the 5-second moment can propel you, give you unexpected insight or clarity, and be an unexpected, pleasant surprise. When I think of small bets and micro actions, I think about taking chances to better myself in the future and working toward goals incrementally.

I've told my kids on more than one occasion that they needed to worry about three people when making decisions: their past self, their present self, and their future self. Like small bets and micro actions, the idea that actions and planning in the present help or hinder you in the future is the idea behind staging.

Staging

Setting yourself up for some future point in time is done in many ways, from buying stocks and investments to taking care of your health and living a life of considerate moderation. From a storytelling perspective, staging opportunities and signs of staging and its benefits can be found everywhere in life. Look for them when engaging in story listening, story creation, and re-storying. In my storyboard, staging is potentially everywhere—at the bottom of ladders or the top, at the top of a chute or the bottom. The idea regarding staging and lending yourself a hand is this: Anytime you get the opportunity to leave yourself a token or Easter egg for your future self to find and use, do it.

Gravity

In the center of the storyboard, there is a picture of a small child and a strange symbol; this is the universal symbol for gravity. The original Chutes and Ladders game board I purchased depicted children throughout the board. One of the first things I did when I began to modify it was to cover each of these pictures with a blank piece of paper using a glue stick. For the child at the center of the board, the piece of paper kept falling off. Coincidence?

Around the time this was happening, I was reading the book *A Short History of Nearly Everything* by Bill Bryson and remembered something he said about gravity and Einstein's theory of space-time. Space-time, Bryson explained, is like a sheet of stretched rubber and items—in this case, planets or our sun—that can stretch the rubber, dependent upon their specific weight, drawing other less heavy objects toward them. Items of lesser weight, then placed upon that sheet, would freely roll toward the heavier body; they would *gravitate* toward it.

As I thought about this astrophysics explanation, my unthinking subconscious mind brought me a thought about the child in the center of my storyboard as a symbol of myself and the idea that we create and attract the world around us. In other words, we have a specific weight and gravity and "pull" things in around us and to us. Suddenly, it seemed intuitively appropriate that my storyboard would have a representative symbol of my original self (a child) at the center, and it certainly seemed as if the universe and unseen forces wanted me to leave that original picture on the board.

The Universe's Ladder and Chute

Earlier in this chapter I discussed self-organizing systems and suggested that the only thing the universe really hates is when you try to control it. Our only job is to create, and then that which we create ultimately controls us. Beyond creating things, we have *intention* and *attention,* and that's about it. When I think about the longest ladder and longest chute on my storyboard, I think about those universal laws. If we are open to what the universe might bring, even if it's different than what we wanted or shows up in a different way, it may be an opportunity to climb to the very top of where we want to go, to clarity and enlightenment. Conversely, if we try to control too much and are not open minded, we may slide back down the chute to our old habits, fears, and beliefs.

Nature of the Game

For me, using this children's game to create a storyboard of my life and journey was ideal. Some final quotes from a famous author sum up life as a game nicely.

According to British-Indian novelist Salmon Rushdie, "All games have morals; and the game of Snakes and Ladders captures, as no other activity can, the eternal truth that for every ladder you climb, a snake is waiting around the corner; and for every snake, a ladder will compensate."

Rushdie went on to say: "It's more than that; this is no mere carrot-and-stick affair; because implicit in the game is the unchanging twoness of things, the duality of up against down, good against evil; the solid rationality of ladders balances the occult sinuosity's of the serpent; in the opposition of staircase and cobra we can see metaphorically, all conceivable oppositions, Alpha against Omega, father against mother."

In closing, the author said he found early in life that the game lacked one crucial dimension, that of ambiguity, because as events show, "It's also possible to slither down a ladder or climb to triumph on the venom of a snake." These quotes illustrate what a great metaphor this game is for life and its struggles, and the last quote encapsulates the purpose of striving to craft a true story in life, one that is ethical, well attended, and cared for with love, patience, and understanding.

Science has yet to explain, and humanity has yet to under-stand, the benefits of living an ethical life. However, if you practice moving through the world tempering your story with empathy, ethics, and morality, you will experience a clearer, more meaningful connection with the universe and create a story to be proud of.

The Multiverse and Grand Unifying Theory

While we're on the subject of life and storytelling, and the universe and how it all might work, I'm excited to say I may have just proved the theory of the multiverse—and while we're at it, perhaps Einstein's grand unifying theory as well. What are they? One is a hypothetical group of multiple universes that together comprise everything, and the other is a model of particle physics that merges all of the universe's three forces (electromagnetic, weak, and strong) into one. Okay, maybe I haven't proven these two theories, but I have a theory that perhaps can point us where to look next—not joking, by the way. The answer lies in one's perspective and the idea that each of us represents a universe unto ourselves. There are those who say multiverse theory is unscientific and cannot be proven, but I think I figured out the answer and it's been right under our noses all the time, literally.

Neuroscientist Rudy Tanzi described the human body and consciousness as a "construct of consciousness," one way in which the universe can order itself into a universe of consciousness comprised of dense information and elements derived from the stars. Hydrogen and nearly all the elements in the human body are also in the cosmos; it is true that we are stardust. Considering that through self-awareness we achieve consciousness and this consciousness in turn creates the reality around us, then each of us can be considered a unique universe unto ourselves. That's my working multiverse theory. What do you think? Although we are a different kind of universe than one composed of stars and planets, we are a densely ordered universe of DNA and bacteria, a conscious construct with self-awareness, and each of us can be thought of as an expression of a unique universe nonetheless.

Albert Einstein was bothered greatly by the idea that he couldn't reconcile the differences between quantum mechanics and general relatively. It bugged him so much in fact that he spent the remainder of his later years trying to join the two, trying to find the connecting link between the apparent conflicting behavior between waves and particles. But what if the missing component to connect these conflicting behaviors is us? What if the link (or lack thereof) is a matter of the observers' perspective, and scaling? Cosmically speaking, we are certainly not the center of the universe when we look to the heavens at night, but we are the centers of *our* individual universes and create a world around us through self-awareness and interpretation.

For Einstein's grand unified theory, we can again apply a simple theory to begin to explain the difference between (particle) quantum mechanics and general relativity wave theory. I pose the two are the same, with the same underlying properties; however, the differences we perceive lie in two things. The first is scaling and the idea there are infinitesimal universes smaller than us existing at atomic and subatomic levels, centrically made of the same components but ordered, focused, and expressed differently. Scaling up infinitely larger than ourselves in the astral plane of the cosmos there are also galaxies and a universe or universes following the same rules. Second, when we as observers "look down" at the atomic level of quantum mechanics, seeing atoms behaving as particles and packets of particles, and then "look up" to the heavens, seeing atoms behaving like connected waves bending space and time, we can't reconcile the two with one another or find a link that connects them.

My working theory on this is that first our limited observer's perspective is an illusion of what our mind perceives when looking from different vantage points. In other words, the two are the same, albeit with differing scales and viewed from different locations. Last, the missing connecting quantum/relativity link is *us* and the fact that humankind has been ordered into a "universe" of consciousness. Einstein left the universe of humanity (us) out of his equations.

So those are my theories on the multiverse and grand unifying theory. Of course, these are working theories and the only purpose of a good theory is to disprove it, taking, as Rudy Tanzi said, what little threads of truth they produce and weaving them into an updated better theory, and then attempting to disprove that one, iteratively. Perhaps there's a bit of tongue-and-cheek to be found in my theories but not too much. The scientific philosopher Karl Popper rejected inductive reasoning (bottom-up logic) in favor of empirical falsification (observing and disproving) and deductive reasoning (top-down logic), in which you start with a premise (theory) and then see if it holds true as you try to disprove it. Popper said, "The only way to test a hypothesis is to look for all the information that disagrees with it." I side with Popper in my reasonings; sorry, Mr. Sherlock Holmes and your deductive reasoning. Lastly, I refer to William of Ockham, 14th century English friar, and his problem-solving principle as the inspiration for my theories. Called *Ockham's razor*, his theory states: "All things being equal, the simplest explanation is usually the correct one." Translation: If it walks like a duck and quacks like a duck, it must be a duck.

Conclusion

If I were to characterize and sum things up, I would say I've started you down a thought path you probably hadn't considered, the idea that stories are everywhere and connect all of us, and everything. You're now likely to start noticing them, looking for them, even telling and creating them. Life would be simpler if we were one-dimensional creatures moving through the world with one single, physical story. However, we're not quite that simple; we have self-awareness and as a result experience consciousness, and this gives us the ability to simultaneously experience multiple planes of existence—the physical, the mental, the spiritual—and with them individual realities and stories or pieces of stories. Thanks to modern technology and digitization, we can now have multiple identities existing in created electronic personas, and each of these can have a story. Whether this leads to a troubling "digifrenia" of fragmented stories or creates a new evolutionary multi "story-verse," I cannot say. Only time will tell.

What I can say about stories is that as we simultaneously live out multiple realities, we pull everything in at an interesting intersection, a juxtaposition between the physical, the mental, and the spiritual. Stories and storytelling are also the perfect human regulators; they provide empathy and an ethical governor to regulate human action that other traditional systems like money and commerce could never provide. Storytelling establishes the truest intention a governing system could bring: the intention, care for, and focus on one other. Supporting a compromise between rational and normative, it is perhaps the most genuine operating system from which to engage in work and life.

Most people today have little idea of their story, the stories around them, or how profoundly they're being influenced by them. As a species, we are simply too distracted, too fragmented, and too diffused to pay attention to such things. We might as well be that fish swimming in the water with no understanding of the environment in which it lives. The connection between storytelling and unthinking is that walking through the world seeing things through a lens of stories and storytelling allows the unthinking intuitive mind and the subconscious to come along with us unencumbered, enriching and clarifying our experience.

The Honest Storyteller

Who is the honest storyteller? Is it the person who courageously bares their soul to a stranger? Is it someone who continuously, even carelessly, exposes themselves for evaluation and judgment, so that others may see and know another's life? Perhaps the honest storyteller isn't human. Perhaps it's the bee pollinating flowers on a spring morning, a fox transitioning through a neighborhood at dawn, the seemingly chaotic social system of birds or any number of wild creatures going about the business of life. I think perhaps the honest storyteller is someone who's true to both them and the world around them with a dual focus on both.

This chapter continues the discussion on storytelling with a look at honesty in storytelling. I began this journey when friends asked me to help them design a storytelling certification program. In 2020 they published their book, *True Storytelling: Seven Principles for an Ethical and Sustainable Change Management Strategy*. A quick Google search on business storytelling produces over 17,000 results. There's a great deal of material on the subject, but a gap existed in books and training about storytelling and leading an ethical life. My friends have created a storytelling manual focused on architecting, living, and working your best life. This is a guide to creating an ethically sustainable and balanced future using true storytelling as a foundation, a foundation from which one can launch and sustain success. Spoiler alert: If you're looking for another marketing program using stories or spoon-fed steps, you won't find it there. This book teaches you how to teach and transform yourself. What you learn becomes yours to keep. Check it out!

Storytelling and Physics

I had another serendipitous moment when I learned about David Bohm, one of the most significant theoretical physicists of the 20th century. I signed up for a webinar offered by SAND (Science and Non-Duality) on the life and ideas of David Bohm, a man Einstein called his "spiritual son" and the Dali Lama said was his "science guru." I had heard Bohm's name associated with other great physicists of the 20th century—Bohr, Einstein, Planck, Oppenheimer, Heisenberg—and I knew Bohm had contributed to the super-secret World War II Manhattan Project (the creation of the atomic bomb) under Oppenheimer, but that was the extent of my knowledge. I knew nothing of Bohm's later work trying to prove the interconnectedness of the universe at the quantum mechanics and general relativity levels.

To my surprise, many of the ideas I mentioned in the last chapter related to proving the multiverse and Einstein's grand unifying theory were also hypothesized by Bohm decades earlier. For me, it was a confirming nod from the universe that I was on to something.

A short video narrated by Guru Krishnamurti explains both the quantum physics and "consciousness" nature of the *observer and the observed* and encapsulates an important idea. The idea is that whatever you observe also becomes part of you. The observer becomes the observed; you change its nature by taking it in, and it changes you in unpredictable and uncontrollable ways. Simply being "aware" of this can save one a lot of conflict in the under-standing, architecting, and living of their own story.

This concept is also tied with quantum mechanics and the famous double slit experiment, in which light acts as either particles or waves depending on whether or not it is being observed. For me, the connection between story creation, physics, and reality is intuitive and powerful. As humans, all of us are privileged with the gift of human consciousness (self-awareness), and whatever we become aware of will also become part of our reality' you might say it also becomes aware of us. Though all of us possess this gift of awareness, we don't experience the same levels of consciousness. Some people are more conscious or aware than others. It also doesn't mean we share the same levels of awareness at the same time. This is dependent upon different factors: the amount of self-reflection we do; our current interests, biases, and experiences; our neurology; whether we feel safe or threatened; and many other factors. Do you remember the funny scene in *Caddyshack* about Bill Murray meeting the Dalai Lama and the prediction he blessed him with? It's worth looking up on the internet. For the benefit of cultivating our best (most honest) true story, simply knowing that the observer *will* become the observed can trigger us to slow down long enough to reflect on experiences, considering the ways they've changed us. This in turn can help us avoid becoming fragmented and isolated and aid in seeing the true nature between things, focusing on the more important realization of our larger life's story—that we are *all* the same connected humans connected to a natural world and universe.

Who Were You When You Woke Up?

The idea is simple: you are most likely on this "story path" called your life completely unaware of your life as a story, and at some point, you wake up to this realization. When this happens, it's important to note that the movie you're currently viewing is unique and specific to that moment. Many variables will come into play: age, geography, socioeconomic factors, etc. The pertinent factors of today weren't the same as those of yesterday or tomorrow. When you wake up to the idea your life is a story being created by you, and cocreated with others, you rise to a new level of consciousness. Awareness and your locus of control shift, and life gets easier and more enjoyable. This is not to say you weren't living a story before this; you just weren't actively creating it.

We are transient beings, so if you don't like who you are, just wait a little while. We've all heard the saying, "same old Bob" and "people don't change." That's very misleading and mostly untrue. It may be comfortable to think that we and others are locked in time, but don't fall for that lazy and limiting belief. We actually do change; we change a lot. As a matter of fact, every cell in our bodies replaces itself about every 7 years. If my 50-something self traveled back in time and met my 20-something self, I'd likely want to punch myself in the face, or at the least give me a stern talking to. Twenty-year-olds are risk takers, egocentric, and enjoy an almost superhuman sense of invulnerability. What does this mean? Just that human consciousness, this gift of self-awareness, is not evenly distributed across our life, and it grows with time and experiences. The next time you run into "same old Bob," ask him how he's the same, or different.

An Honest Walk in the Woods

> "Sometimes a man needs to throw a loaf of bread in a sack and jump over the back fence." —John Muir

A couple of years from now, my son and I are thinking of hiking the Appalachian trail in the Eastern United states, a 6-month thru-hike, which means starting at one end and not stopping until we get to the other side, from Georgia to Maine. Searching for a reason to undertake such an arduous journey, we decided we would do it in honor of our birthdays: I'll be turning 60 and he will be turning 30 on the trail.

But what could possibly be the real reason? I'm currently reading Bill Bryson's book *A Walk in the Woods* and thinking that doing the trail virtually on the internet sounds like a much more comfortable (and maybe smarter) way to go. But if it is smarter, smarter in what way? I would argue that it would certainly be smarter in a tactical, superficial sort of way, but maybe not in a strategic (in the future) way. In true form to our digital age, we could get the data, the information of the trail, faster and from the comfort of our couches, and even skip, fast forward, and multi-task while doing so. But we would miss many complex (even quantum) real connections, and we would miss the time that would pass to process and reflect on what we took in.

In the movie version of Bryson's book, actor Nick Nolte asks Robert Redford: "What gives with you? Do you feel like a caged animal? Is life too perfect and you want to live?" For me, this is what's at the heart of such endeavors. An adventure such as this is part physics, exploring that quantum connection and examining the idea that all things are truly connected on a deeper level; it's part opportunity to connect with my son on a deeper level; and it's an opportunity to add to our stories and add a capstone to life. Update: At the time of editing this, Anthony and I had completed our first 250 miles of the Appalachian Trail and the experience was amazing. Catch my LinkedIn articles on the experience if you want to know more.

History of the Storyteller

In *The Storyteller*, Walter Benjamin suggested that the invention of the novel was the beginning of the end for storytelling. But as we began to trade the art of oral storytelling for the written word, did we discard or just change storytelling? Storytelling is a social and cultural activity, with most stories containing practical information. Usefulness and helpfulness may be the true nature of any story and the most ethical and honest component. Researchers have suggested that stories and language began with useful and practical information, and even social and helpful gossip was meant to teach with an orientation toward practical interests. Benjamin said, "Stories contain, either overtly or covertly, something useful in the form of a moral, proverb, maxim, or practical advice."

Are we losing our patience for talk? Some would disappointedly say yes while others would happily say yes as they prefer reading, listening, and watching to live human discourse and interaction. This trend is growing. Today, we like to turn on the television to hear a story, but that's one-way communication requiring little cognitive effort. What do we lose when we give this up? Moving away from shared oral stories is moving us closer to isolation and a world lived solely in our heads. Benjamin said the storyteller is a man who has counsel for his listeners and honors the story by putting it above himself. If we no longer have counsel for others, can we have it for ourselves and our story?

Benjamin ultimately argues that nothing happening now benefits storytelling. Instead, it benefits information, which is "shot through with explanation," leaving little room for human experience, growth, or learning. And the value of information, he said, does not survive the moment in which it was new.

Honest Stories and Business

"Once there was a boy who had no immunity against disease and lived inside a plastic bubble. Isolated and alone, everything he consumed or read or played with was given to him through a sealed opening; otherwise he would be contaminated and die. As he deteriorated, it became clear he was dying. Knowing this, he asked if he could touch his father outside of the bubble, even though it would mean death. He reached outside and touched his father's hand."
—John Travolta, *The Boy in the Plastic Bubble*, 1976

"High-tech must accompany high touch." In the story above, friend Graham Williams, management consultant, executive coach, and owner of the popular *Storytelling in Business* blog, asked: "Is the loss of the habit of storytelling resulting in the equivalent of this story?" Touch can be a tool of mindful presence, emotional intelligence, empathy, and compassion, and the skin is our biggest sensory organ. Is it being deprived? The rise of technology creating a fourth industrial revolution, combined with the recent pandemic crisis, has created more data, more information, and more isolation.

What Graham characterized as "clicks and bricks" combined with social distancing has creating a threat and fear of others. Tech and COVID-19 have driven us away from one another. Prior to the pandemic, information and communications technology was already resulting in a measure of social isolation and distancing and impacting meaningful community relationship building. This trend is set to increase with the advent of the fourth industrial revolution that includes robotics, artificial intelligence, and fifth-generation telecommunications and data. This will further impact our attention spans, isolation, and loneliness, a trend that may well have been hastened by the arrival of COVID-19.

Humankind has continuously adapted and evolved. As social beings, we group together for protection and advancement. Closeness and physical proximity are part of our DNA and beneficial to our physical immune systems and our emotional, social, and spiritual well-being. Graham argued that we need to beware of losing touch and begin telling a different story—one of connection, not separation; closeness, not distance; and compassion, not fear. Live communication is a critical function of the words we exchange. How we use and 'read' body language, expressions, voice tone, pitch, and volume, as well as our matching and mirroring and the activation of mirror neurons during conversations are vital to our survival as a species. Before we hasten from what we did yesterday to what we will do now and tomorrow, we must consider where we have been, lest we lose ourselves.

Storytelling as a Profession

There are professions which use (or should use) storytelling, and law is one that immediately comes to mind. Lawyers need to be natural storytellers, and a good lawyer can uncover and present a human story while also pulling together the facts and comparing them to the law. My neighbor, retired lawyer John Tanner, said: "Storytelling in the law is important but is complicated by the equal importance of facts (helpful and unhelpful) and the law itself. Legal elements usually involve multiple factors, and the temptation is to organize a case around these elements and to introduce facts only as they bear on legal elements. This approach, however, creates a disjointed narrative and usually omits unhelpful facts." John said the storytelling approach involves setting out *all* the facts up front and telling a story with them. This approach is easy to follow and welcomes the highlighting of helpful facts. Equally important, it permits putting unhelpful facts in context, and in the best light; everyone has a full view of what happened. Done in this way, the unhelpful facts are laid to rest and the parties are receptive to a discussion of the elements. This telling amounts to a retelling of your story from a new perspective, and the legal arguments become self-evident. John, a native of North Carolina, is a master storyteller (a prerequisite for such a birthing, I suppose) and as a recovering lawyer he now spends his time these days searching for, and disputing, the best BBQ in the country. Catch his great BBQ restaurant blog online. My stomach uses it every summer as navigational coordinates to some of the best hole in the wall BBQ joints around, "I rest my case!"

The Thoughtfully Curated Story

I don't know to what extent storytelling is taught in law schools, but in my opinion every university with a law program should have a robust storytelling curriculum. I met Diane Wyzga several years ago and was instantly drawn to her thoughtfully curated life and story. She's a person who has developed a niche where the universe needs one. From registered nurse to business-person to lawyer to legal consultant and now storyteller and professional wordsmithing coach, Diane consults and teaches story-telling. She has a successful podcast with global followership entitled *Stories from Women Who Walk*, where she shares wisdom and interviews geared toward helping others become successful storytellers, story creators, and succeed in business.

Among my favorites is *My Life as Compost*, episode #103, where Diane says, "The smelly garbage in your life is stuff that's meant to grow you; it's your compost." In the podcast, *Is It Lying or Storytelling*, episode #104, Diane asked, "What's the difference between lying and storytelling?" To respond, she quoted Diane

Setterfield: "Storytelling is a way of telling the truth; lying is an attempt to conceal the truth. Storytelling benefits the community, lying benefits the liar. Storytelling is a gift while lying is an act of thievery. Storytelling invites the listener to apply their intelligence; lying is an effort to keep him or her in ignorance. Storytelling is a mutual engagement with rules; lying is a one-sided exploitation."

In *What's Your Business Backstory*, episode #91, Diane stated that an "untold story is a burden." To lighten the burden by creating a story involves "listening for the story that wants to be told." The best storytellers are a conduit for the story that wants to be told. The best businesses know that a heartfelt story artfully told will bring their vision, purpose, or mission statement to life, intuitively inspiring the action they want others to take.

What's your business's, and life's, story? A story engages the right side of the brain, allowing listeners to put themselves into it. The right brain invites the story in, along with the facts and information the left brain wants, and then empathetically relates to it, putting you in the story. Diane says: "We know what we know, when that feeling hits, you listen to it and honor it." Visit Diane at *Quarter Moon Story Arts* and listen in while she helps socially conscious professional women and entrepreneurs develop their story message to amplify their values, purpose, and vision. I suspect it won't be long before we're listening to Diane's wisdom on NPR.

"Pilgrim, there is no path. The path is made by walking. By walking you make the path." —Antonio Machado

There's a danger in going your own way and also reward in purposefully creating your own story. I feel the need to warn you about both. Then if you are motivated enough by this book to drop everything and make a major course correction, you will know the good and the bad.

The story of physicist David Bohm is an exemplar of the dangers of following your own path and, conversely, the reward of a story well lived. Truth be told, I would strongly advise you to write (live) your own story, omitting whatever doesn't support, encourage, or grow you. You've heard the saying, "Go where you're celebrated, not tolerated." That's my advice.

For me, Bohm's story is a remarkable one for several reasons. First, I feel a deep connection to Bohm's work in quantum physics, the nature of reality, and human consciousness. I feel that Bohm was on the verge of discovering something remarkable for mankind when he died. When I think of Bohm's work, I'm reminded of the words of the late Wayne Dyer, who said, "When you change the way you look at things, the things you look at change." Next, I feel empathetic to the story of Bohm's life. He suffered an unhappy childhood growing up in a coal-mining town during the Depression. His father wanted him to take over the family appliance store but David was not interested—being more interested in science, to his father's disappointment. Eventually David became estranged from his father and was accepted to Penn State University, Berkeley, and Princeton. Because of his exceptional marks, he got his first job at Princeton University under the tutelage of physicist Robert Oppenheimer, who became a surrogate father. There he became a member of the Manhattan Project under Oppenheimer, wrote a highly regarded book on quantum theory, taught, and was befriended by Albert Einstein.

He wrote several breakthrough research papers in his lifetime, one of which, "Hidden Variables," got him ostracized from the physics orthodoxy. It attempted to reconcile Einstein's grand unifying theory, which tried to find the link between quantum mechanics and general relativity and hinted at the idea of an overall connecting consciousness in the universe at the quantum level—an undivided wholeness he later called the *implicate* (unfolded) *order* from which all things in the universe originated. Bohm theorized this world we live in and everything in it represented an explicate (folded) order, all coming from the deeper implicate order, a level in which all things were connected.

Bohm was ostracized by Oppenheimer over the article. Oppenheimer instructed the physics community that if they couldn't disprove Bohm's hidden variables paper, then Bohm must instead be ignored. Bohm moved to England heartbroken. Although he continued his contributions as physicist, he spent the remainder of his years researching the links between quantum mechanics, human consciousness, and the philosophy of the mind. In the 1980s, Bohm's forgotten hidden variables paper was rediscovered by a new group of young physicists and definitively proven at Birkbeck University where he taught. Using new computer-generated models, Bohm was able to see for the first time what he had theoretically proposed decades earlier. He was ecstatic.

All the data is not yet in on the specific dangers of living *your* own personal story (and I am currently in the middle of mine). However, if I were to guess, I would say the perils of going your own honest way are that you will likely experience a surprising and sometimes bumpy ride to a satisfying destination.

Honest Questions and Dialogue—The Secret to Life

Bohm's later research at the intersection of quantum mechanics and human consciousness cultivated a friendship with Indian spiritualist Krishnamurti that produced 22 years of productive discussions in human consciousness and physics. These discussions are largely centered around the concept of the *observer and the observed*. It's the idea that what we observe influences and changes us and, by virtue of this, we change it.

During one of these discussions, however, Krishnamurti said something subtle but very profound regarding the nature of another subject: asking questions. It's a theme I've heard only once before from one of my mentors on learning, Dr. Michael Marquardt, and relates to the transformative power of asking questions. Mike said that from the moment we are born, we have two critical objectives as a matter of survival—to learn to walk and to learn to talk—and we undertake these tasks in earnest. The problem, he says, comes when inquisitive children are told by their parents and society to "stop asking so many questions." When this happens, sincere and honest inquisition and dialogue take a big hit.

Bringing back this dialogue and reestablishing this rapid method of growth and learning for businesses and individuals has been the focus of Mike's life's work. The World Institute for Action Learning was cofounded by Mike to help organizations come up with breakthrough strategies to urgent problems, develop leaders of everyone in a group, and build high-performing teams. It's an amazing process. Action learning is now practiced in over 150 countries around the world.

As the story goes between Bohm, Krishnamurti, and questions, each scientist depended on the other's questioning to bring out their inspiration and brilliance. They both felt strongly that they had valuable knowledge and insights locked inside of them which only questions and Bohm-style dialogue (bohemian dialogue) could bring forward. As storytelling has also shown, when we share stories, we also invite questions of ourselves and others, and this promotes new learning, discovery, contribution, and inspiration.

The Tragedy of Life

If there is a tragedy in life, perhaps it is that we have been cognitively out of balance (and disconnected) for centuries and it feels as if the pendulum may never swing back toward center. This adds unnecessary anxiety, grief, pain, and suffering to every subsequent generation of humanity. There has been a struggle between the rational and the intuitive mind going back as far as the 15th century, perhaps further, arguing and fighting for a left- or right-brained point of view, a mechanical or natural world view. This continues today as we look for and crave perfection in information and data. Its promise is intoxicating, yet perfection in the natural world is not mechanical but transient, fleeting, contextual, and changing. It's alive, not a snapshot; it's a forest in the rain, not a map with names on it. Einstein said, "The rational mind is a humble servant, the intuitive mind is a sacred gift, we have created a society that honors the servant and has forgotten the gift." And the promise of the rational mind still alludes us to this day. Even with ever increasing advances in science we still use rational discoveries to irrational ends and cannot eradicate things like poverty, racism, disease, or war. Finally, it's not only tragic that we might never become undistracted enough from the relentless persistence of the rational left brain and the march of technology to pay attention to and cultivate our own stories, connecting them with the world. It's that we won't teach it to our children because no one taught it to us, we wouldn't know what to teach. We won't teach the reflective exercise of being aware and stitching together the random experiences of life and the connectedness of all things into a meaningful narrative. A friend recently commented that "all the random events of life don't seem to connect." How do we connect seemingly unrelated experiences throughout life, what's the connection and should they be connected? Can we stitch them together into a story leading to a destination of satisfaction and fulfillment? The answer is yes, they are already connected, and the connection is us. They may not connect themselves in our minds unless we spend the time to do so; that time would be well spent.

End of a Story

What does this all mean, for the individual living their story or the organization trying to stitch together a story which is true for its members? Just this; as my friend Richard Herder Professor of Communication at Southwest Minnesota State University put it to me "Stories are at the heart of everything." The march of technology and human endeavor is accelerating in a world already careening out of balance, it will go on. Facts, figures, data, calculation, we have a love affair with these external (explicate "folded" order) things. We see them in front of us and therefore see them as a logical panacea, but they're not. Though they're meant to serve us, on their own they provide no room for the human condition and our deep desire to connect, relate, be heard, be helpful, and feel loved, we add that distinction, and room. Facts, figures, and data only achieve purpose, legitimacy, and honor when baked into the human story. No matter how brief or subtle that story is, to omit this ingredient is like leaving the baking powder out of a cake, it doesn't produce anything and doesn't connect anywhere. When we seek only data from the world, we seek it for its own purpose, and when we do that, we forget its true purpose. We forget the people it's meant to serve and make *it* the master instead of ourselves. And in doing so we leave no room for learning, possibilities, questions, and discovery. We forfeit our honest selves, discard life for the lifeless and honor a thing which has no value.

Defining and Refining Our Stories

Let's make late physicist David Bohm our guide as we define and refine the story of our lives on a path to unlocking and channeling our intuitive unthinking minds. I'll help David by sharing four pieces of his advice (along with some of my own), which you can incorporate to channel the best of human consciousness into your life. Together, we will cover the most important considerations you will ever have to decide in life.

In this life, we are constantly aware of what Bohm calls the *explicate* (unfolded) *order*. That's where our consciousness *is* and *dwells* every day. What is it? It's the things all around us, the stuff we see daily, and it can be pervasive, in your face, alluring, and confusing. It's preoccupying for most, and all-consuming for some. It can occupy us for a lifetime and keep us off higher tasks like *story caretaking*.

What's story caretaking? It's a type of self-curation in which we select, pull together, sift through, and share the best of what it is to be us. It's caring for a story not only for us but also for others. Perhaps as a testament to the sometimes contradiction of life, this consciousness which gives us the gift of self-awareness and is preoccupied with the external world is also our connection to the implicate order, the foundation underneath and the unthinking subconscious intuitive mind.

Connect to Wholeness

Every day we live in the explicate order, the external world, but how do we connect with the undivided wholeness of an implicate order, a shared connection? The answer is deceptively simple. One way is by communing with one another through dialogue. When we collectively ask questions, we share meaning and begin to ask better and better questions as we learn more about others and, in turn, ourselves. From it we potentially pull better and better answers and deeper meaning from the implicate order. That's one way.

In your work and your personal life, coworkers and acquaintances can come and go, and mostly they're collaborators of one sort or another. You tacitly or explicitly agree to work on a job and through discussion and effort you hammer it out. But occasionally you connect with someone on a deeper cooperative level. When this happens, mechanical "discussion" (a word that rhymes with *percussion* and *concussion*) changes and turns to dialogue, a word whose origins are with the prefix *dia* (to pass through) and *logos* (to share meaning). What might have been a "ping-pong game"–like exchange, a discussion, perhaps to defend a position, gain advantage, or get information, becomes a sharing of meaning and a growing experience for everyone involved. Instead of forcing, wrenching, or mechanically going through motions executing protocols and processes, you learn together and, equally important, you *learn how to learn* together. When this happens, everything you produce will feel like a quantum leap from where you've been, an order of magnitude better. When meaning flows through people, we are connected to Bohm's undivided wholeness, the implicate order, the collective base from which all things originate.

The second way to connect is more personal and involves clearing a path to wholeness. I recently met an educator named Tramaine Crawford who has devoted his professional and personal life to empowering Black youth in America. Tramaine caught my eye when he said that children become what they see. That's a great statement. From birth, we pull our reality from the explicate order, the external world. What we see and hear surrounds us with what we define as reality. These structures become our world and, at least for a time, we may know no other. While it's true we're always connected with the implicate order and wholeness through thoughts and reflection and may even share meaning and understanding from it with those close to us, rare is the child who can make sense of connecting with wholeness once society fills their subconscious with things from the external world.

One of the most limiting and distressing shortcomings of our external (explicate order) world is the objectifying and fragmenting nature of nearly all things in it. As an example, a descriptive phrase such as "I am" would make no sense in our divided world of today without a delineating noun or adjective accompanying it: *I am Eric; I am a man,* etc. However, this is precisely what God was alleged to have said in the Christian Bible to Moses when Moses asked him his name. The inference is that God's reply of "I am" meant he was limitless and without description, connected to everything in an undivided wholeness. This certainly does not feel like the case with us and the world today as everything we see, touch, hear, and feel is specifically defined, divided, individual and separate. Our lives are subject to self-imposed boundaries and borders, dividing states, countries, ethnicities, genders, social classes, everything. And these divisions are created by us; they not part of a natural world.

I've not yet had the opportunity to talk with Tramaine about how he's guiding and empowering his kids using books to build their own stories. When we do talk, I will tell him that while it's true children become what they see, they also see with their minds as well as their eyes. This eyesight is guided from an undivided implicate order we're all connected to. This is the power in what he's doing. Contradiction, conflict, incoherence, fragmentation, isolation—these are challenges encountered in the explicate, external order of our outside world. While there can be no other way than for humans to live in both worlds, there is a way to live in which we master one while staying connected to the other.

How can we feel this connection to wholeness? My friend Julia Hayden in her book *Gaia Dialogue* introduced me to a phenomenon astronauts' experience called the *overview effect*. It's a phenomenon in which witnessing the world from outer space causes a cognitive shift, giving one a feeling of unified connectedness to one global home. We don't have to be astronauts to experience this transformative effect. We might feel this wholeness by practicing lucid dreaming (something I've had some success with), or we may develop our everyday perception enough to sense a connection in our waking day at will.

Wholeness Arises Between Us

Wholeness is not exclusively yours or mine. You won't be able to hold on to it on your own, at least not for long. It's on loan to us, and like a subscription must be paid into and renewed. Have you ever noticed how sometimes solutions to problems magically appear? There's no magic to it at all, and if you trace back far enough you will discover its origins came after talking within a group or listening to a story or a friend and reflecting. Your connection to wholeness within the implicate order has produced these answers. We never come up with breakthrough strategies alone, so before mentally bragging about your singlehanded accomplishment think of its origins.

Human consciousness comes hardwired with a connection to the undivided whole Bohm speaks of, the implicate order. Every day when we wake, our consciousness has a clear connection to it, then it's downhill from there. I'm kidding, of course, but only a little: Things don't necessarily degrade the moment the external world begins to come in, crowd out, and dilute our connection to the implicate order, but it certainly adds layers of complexity we should be aware of. Interestingly, Bohm said that we "follow a pattern of enfoldment and unfoldment," moving forward and back, in and out, or between the two.

As we unfold into the explicate order of the day, we're often carried away and affirmed with individualism, separateness, and uniqueness, to the satisfaction of the ego. A big part of our psyche and consciousness, the ego is an abstraction whose charge is to validate this individuality and uniqueness and to protect us, especially when we are young and vulnerable. Our mind is always connected to the implicate order, but it's the pursuit of, and attendance to, abstractions and objects in the explicate, with delegation and curation from the ego, which lead us through most days, and most of our troubles.

Seek Coherence

The second piece of advice is to seek coherence—and avoid incoherence. Bohm said our main source of unhappiness is that we are incoherent and therefore producing results we don't really want. We then spend a great deal of time fretting and trying to overcome these problems while simultaneously continuing to produce them, never realizing the cycle we are in. Often, we don't make logical sense, we don't have clear connections, and we are disjointed and unhappy.

How can we avoid incoherence? One way is to avoid isolation. Incoherence flourishes in isolation. In isolation there is fragmentation (a word meaning both separated and broken). Wholeness, if you can achieve it, Bohm said, is not a physical place you can get to like heaven (if you believe in the concept of heaven). It's an attitude and approach toward the whole of life. If we can practice coherence, the universe will respond coherently to us in kind. The solutions we collectively pull from the implicate order, together, using questions and dialogue, lead to coherence and wholeness. Wholeness, Bohm said, "arises *between us in participation,*" not from individuals in isolation.

Coherence and Leaders

One thing great leaders have in common is coherence. They espouse a life of connectedness and logical thinking; these are simple messages from the implicate order. Universal messages like these are always glaringly obvious in terms of their value and transformative power, and just as frequently they're ignored, hastily dismissed, and overlooked for the fragmented divided trappings of the explicate order. What are these recurring messages from history's most sage leaders? They are usually to seek wholeness (unity), compassion, and a connected purpose with everything.

Throughout the centuries advice and examples have come in the form of stories illustrating in detail how to clearly walk that path. God, Jesus, Buddha, Lao-tzu, Muhammad, Gandhi, the Dalai Lama—it doesn't matter what wise leader you cite, they all caveat their messages with "try and do your best." The idea here is that you won't succeed in being exactly like me or doing exactly what I do, these leaders note. At this task you'll fail and that's okay. What's most important is to try, be aware. This is another powerful message of the implicate "enfolded "order where connection is what matters. In this realm we succeed with effort, not perfection.

To be better at the end is a byproduct of connection with others. Simply to try is success and creates tremendous energy.

With fragmentation and division, however, comes incoherence. And with the isolation the explicate order of the external world brings, there's often confusion and a muddled message interpreted from some of our leaders. Some messages have sent nations to war, caused humans to hate, and caused the natural world to retreat and shrink from abuse and indifference. What are these incoherent and irrational messages we often reflect back from our wisest? Unfortunately, the message we think we hear isn't "try" or "do your best" or "keep an open mind." Instead it's "do exactly as I do," "look exactly like me," and "think exactly as I think." And "there is no other way." The incoherence of a beautiful message corrupted is caused by the filtering of it through the two worlds, the implicate and the explicate. One world professes and assures abundance and the other scarcity; one is grounded in connection and wholeness, and the other in separation and division.

Why don't we see the error of this incoherence, which causes nature and humanity to suffer endlessly, and reverse it? Why don't we follow the *true* advice? Perhaps it's because our conflicted human nature simultaneously wants to connect with others and be isolated, or perhaps it's conditioning, bias, or evolution. Or maybe we too "enfold and unfold" like waves on a beach rolling back and forth. I think perhaps it's a little bit of everything. Whatever the reasons, it is why we achieve remarkable rational answers in science, religion, and philosophy, only to execute them in irrational or destructive ways. To manage and honor your story best, understand your human nature *and* your human limits, and those of others. Understand your part in the play, as William Shakespeare once said, and the reality that you are an actor in your play and in others' plays. Play your best.

Incoherence, Self-Deception, and Delusion

The observable world we live in is largely an abstraction. What does that mean? It means that despite the idea, the certainty even, that this world we touch, feel, and see is 100% concrete and the same to everyone, it's really a made-up interpretation unique to us alone. It's uniquely translated, filtered, and sorted by each of us through 188 known human biases, over 100,000 years of evolution and preprogrammed tapes written decades ago or even at birth and unknown to us. The bottom line is the end solution we live and experience is a reality that, while similar to others, is unique to only us. This sounds like it could be a lonely place to exist if we let it. What is real, however, is the connectedness we share in the implicate order. That connection, though sometimes blocked, is always coupled. And what of the delineation, individualism, uniqueness, and separation we scratch, claw, compete, fight for, see, and encounter everywhere in the world? Bohm said that's not real either. We're all connected—to each other, to the planet and its inhabitants, and to the universe.

Maybe it occurred to you while we have been having this discussion that the practice of unthinking can keep that channel to the implicate order clear more often for us. If you had that thought, you're right. It's a reciprocal process. Not only does exercising, using the intuitive, gut-feeling, subconscious part of our brain and bodies (there are also neural cells in our hearts and stomachs) open our unthinking powers and abilities, connecting us more often to Bohm's implicate order, but also the more often we're aware of our connection, the stronger and sharper our unthinking abilities and gifts become. And how exactly do we start practicing unthinking other than stopping our delusion and self-deception and becoming more coherent? And how exactly do you do those things? I could probably sell a million copies of this little book if I were to lay out step-by-step unthinking instructions, provide numbered checklist steps, or offer pithy advice on how to unthink, but I'd probably be doing us both a grave disservice and would likely be deceptive to boot, as unthinking is going to be a different experience for everyone. (Remember our discussion about us as individual universes and realities?) The bottom line is you've got to sort out the specific details, figure it (unthinking) out, and experience it for yourself or it won't work and become a way of life, and it won't stick. But as I've hinted, suggested, speculated, and asked about how to do it throughout this book, I am comfortable offering ways and steps to prepare an environment for unthinking—to host, encourage, and promote it. It starts with doing things like suspending judgment, staving off decisions until they have to be made, and asking thoughtful questions. This gives the intuitive mind time to process and contribute to the experiences unfolding. Here are a few more suggestions to consider and ideas to try. And hey, maybe I'll still sell a million copies and make some wider connections in the process.

Get a Weltanschauung

Pronounced *vel-tun-shou-un,* this is the German word for "worldview" and means "a comprehensive conception or image of the universe" and of humanity's relation to it. Your story *must* have a worldview, a philosophy and conception of life.

Where do worldviews come from? They may come from science, religion, or philosophy, depending upon your preferences and biases. Does your mind like to drill down to objective facts and data or take in a big picture view? To the science minded, the mechanistic, or the object driven, hard data, facts, and measurement might be a pleasing worldview. To the religious, the philosophical, the abstract, or those who prefer people to things, a larger, more subjective 10,000-foot picture might be more comforting and relatable, and they might have more tolerance for things like complexity, divergence, and ambiguity.

Keep your mind open to specific worldviews and concepts. Just because we put our trust in a specific scientific method of the day doesn't necessarily mean it's the best way or that it's the right way. We intuit that it is best—that measurement is the best way to determine an objective world, for example. But even rationality is grounded in an intuitive hunch that behaving rationally is the best thing to do. Hundreds of years ago, science was different than it is today and was conducted differently. Originally what is now referred to as the "hard sciences" was once called "natural philosophy" and included room for things, thoughts, and hypotheses that could not be easily reduced to equations, even things that included art and emotion. The bottom line is that today's science is nothing more than our current "best guess" at things, not an objective final answer.

Quantum physics has shown us that when we think we discover the basic building blocks of life (atoms, for example), they recede as we discover a finer constitution beyond them (molecules, atoms, neutrons, protons, etc.). Even today, though, we hold the title of "PhD" above reproach; we curiously overlook that it stands for "doctor of philosophy." What I'm saying is that we don't know everything, and we will never reach an end to learning and discovery. It's bottomless.

Your story needs to be like this too. Engineer your story in a way that you are not only okay with this idea of endless learning but also conduct yourself accordingly. Be open-minded and leave room for learning. One problem with a worldview grounded only in science is that the sciences of today tend to break up every new discovery, separate and divide it, classifying each part as individual and unrelated to other sciences. While attempts are periodically made to unify the different sciences and discoveries, things in our world are hopelessly separated. As your story enfolds and unfolds from the implicate to the explicate and back again, make your best guess on things using science, religion, philosophy, or whatever you have at hand. Remember, when we unfold our stories together from the implicate order with dialogue, it comes from pure wholeness.

Recognize That It's Not All About You

I've got some bad news, some good news, and some great news.

The bad news? I'm not sure how to put this so I'll just say it: your story isn't about you. That's bad news for your ego, which is not going to take it well. So how can the story of your life be *your* story and not be about *you*? It's simple. Your story *includes* you, but you aren't the center of it (or at least you shouldn't be). Think about it: you wouldn't exist as you are in your current configuration without *everything* and *everyone* else in it. Instead of thinking of yourself as the sole proprietor of *you*, think of yourself as the property of others and as your story's steward, caretaker, and gardener. Manage and tend this story carefully and meticulously for someone else, for others, or even *something* else, like a passion or cause. In one of his conversation lectures, physicist David Bohm pointed out that there is a great difference between passions and desires. Desires, he said, invest (and waste) your energy in explicative external ways, towards abstractions, objects, and things. Passion, by comparison, channels tremendous energy beyond oneself and towards a higher connected purpose.

The good news? When you see your life in this way, the tumblers on the cosmic lock will turn and open to a new view of the world, and you will be able to see farther than you could before.

What's the great news? This is how things are meant to be, so when you start to incorporate these principles, the universe will recognize this clearer connection to wholeness and respond in kind. You'll begin to behave more coherently, creating more of the things you want in life and less of the things you don't. It's a synergistic circle spiraling up. You'll start to experience synchronicities. Your intuition (your unthinking mind) will check in with you more and your amygdala less, and serendipity will come to call more often.

Acknowledge your connection to others with dialogue and awareness and share your story. Put it out there for others to see and be inspired by. You'll feel less alone and more often heard and needed.

An Introduction to Hard Things

It's early December in the mountains of Spokane, Washington, just 3 weeks before Christmas. I was a young U.S. Air Force sergeant at Fairchild Air Force Base attending its wilderness survival school. We were in our fifth day in the woods, and it had been snowing most of the day. A fresh 6 inches of new fallen snow now covered the already foot and a half lying on the ground. Our thrown-together team of four aircrew members representing four different branches of military service plus one survival school instructor was beleaguered and beset with troubles. There wasn't a single part of us which wasn't wet and cold. Chills ran through our bodies in waves like tremors. We were dirty, smelled of smoke, and were hungry. Night was the worst.

Our course scenario was simple; we had parachuted behind enemy lines into hostile territory and had to get across the border to be repatriated with our units. This particular night, we had heard through intercepted radio transmissions that enemy forces were in the area and looking for *us*. That meant we couldn't have the warm campfire we had on previous nights; the light and smoke would be easily detected. Huddling together that evening around a 1-foot hole dug in the ground with a single candle in the bottom, we took in whatever warmth we could get from this survival fire. It was the lowest part of our journey.

As we crouched in the silence, shivering, sniffling, gazing down into the single flame, we listened to the wind in the trees and an owl hooting in the distance. Our survival school instructor broke the silence, leaned in, and spoke. "Pull in close," he said. "I want to tell you something. I'm going to give you some advice, something you can take with you the rest of your lives, something which will serve you and help you no matter what situation you are in, no matter where you are." We drew in closer, and the air seemed to get sucked out of our small circle. I wasn't aware of anything at that moment except my instructor's face in the flickering candlelight. He looked at each of us slowly, locking eyes, and said these words: "Learn to tolerate discomfort." Those words, so ordinary, even ridiculous, took on a meditative state in that moonlight and gave each of us new strength beyond our past capabilities. Those four simple words have stayed with me for decades. It's been almost 30 years now and the sergeant's advice still comes back to help me at unexpected moments, large and small.

What Are Hard Things?

Hard things are not what you might think they are. They're not the things we actively avoid for fear of pain or discomfort—the college degrees, the promotion interviews, the addictions. More insidious than that, they're the frets, worries, stressors, and unconscious things baked into our DNA, which most of us are never aware of and never reconcile. Let's look at the biological stressors that can unknowingly plague us for a lifetime. To know our enemies is to make peace with them.

Control

We've got serious control issues. Talk to almost any middle-aged man in America and you're likely to see what I mean. Control can be great, but it becomes a problem when it leaves its own swim lane and ventures into others' waters. And it does this all the time, causing tremendous stress both for the recipient of the control attempts and the controller. Whether it's individuals, governments, or society, control imposed on others is seldom virtuous, productive, or welcomed.

To conquer your need to control people or situations, ask where the impulse is coming from. What's behind it? Why? You may find it is grounded in baseless fear or from your past. Next, to come to terms with a desire for external control, consider that the only thing we really have control over in life is our own thoughts and actions. Trying to extend your reach beyond that would likely be frustrating folly. Additionally, with 188 currently known human biases and a subconscious that (unconsciously) directs 80% of our waking day with what you've done in the past, you'd be hit and miss at trying to predict and direct the thoughts and behaviors of another. You'd also be a hypocrite, so figure yourself out first before you try to control anyone else.

Certainty

We want certainty in life, but we'll never have it 100%; get used to that. Like control, the closest to securing certainty we'll ever get is our own self-governance. Even then, anything could happen along the way. As researcher Karl Weick once said, "How do I know what I think until I see what I've said?" In other words, the reality of the present isn't certain until it's being committed to the past.

Recently I had a great conversation with a friend about developing leadership skills. They confessed they struggled with ambiguity, and it was one of their stressors, adding that they had much work yet to do in overcoming that challenge. In my estimation, their work has already begun in earnest, and they are probably handling their ambiguity with uncertainty in the most efficient way possible. When we set our intention to do something, practicing or thinking of it once or twice and then letting it slip from the conscious mind, we may think it goes away, but it really doesn't. It goes into our mind's vast subconscious and the work continues there. Your subconscious mind is always working, problem solving, relating, and looking for connections. It's like when you're thinking of buying a Prius automobile and suddenly you see Priuses everywhere. Your subconscious hasn't forgotten your original intention or question. Grappling with certainty, uncertainty, and ambiguity is best thought of and handled in similar fashion: "set it and forget it," have the initial thought, ask the question, and then let it go. An intuitive answer will soon come back. That's the power of the unthinking mind.

Boredom (and Patience)

One Sunday morning not long ago, I was feeling bored, impatient, and aggravated. It was an uncomfortable and stressful feeling. I was conflicted: part of me wanted to continue doing nothing, or nothing constructive, and part of me wanted to force productive behavior from the morning (like finishing this chapter you're reading) even though that felt impossible because I didn't have any ideas about what to write next. Interestingly, and as if in some universal serendipity, I turned on my favorite Sunday morning show, *CBS Sunday Morning,* and the first human interest news story that aired was the very thing I needed to round out my thoughts. According to Dr. Amit Sood, professor at the Mayo Clinic, the opposite of patience isn't impatience; the opposite of patience is *anger, anxiety, illness, injury, addiction, loneliness,* and even *death.* Impatience causes stress, and this is an uncomfortable part of our nature. We are designed this way out of survival; it's one reason babies cry. But becoming overly stressed or angry can increase your risk of sudden death as much as eightfold.

People have a very hard time understanding what they *do* and *do not* have control over, but practicing *resilience,* the ability to respond to and readily recover from a crisis, can help you tackle impatience. It has to do with your locus of control, either internal or external, and you can get better at it with practice. Resilience boosts our immune cells.

Nature can help us master impatience, strengthening resilience. One invention of the Japanese, forest bathing, or hiking in slow motion, quietly taking in everything around you, builds resilience. Walking in nature for 15 minutes lowers blood pressure and decreases stress hormones like cortisol. We've all heard the expression "don't let life pass you by." Have you ever stopped to wonder what that means? While on the surface it sounds like a warning that we're moving too slowly and life is passing us, it's actually a warning that we're moving too fast; life is surpassing us. It sounds like an oxymoron but it's not: it's a call to slow down and practice some empathetic patience. Hiking 250 miles of the Appalachian Trail with my son in the spring of 2022 brought that point home for both of us. Eventually we plan to hike the entire trail in sections.

Focus

Buddhists have an expression, "monkey mind." It's the description of a restless brain that can't focus and is in a perpetual state of distraction, jumping, swinging. Like impatience, this is also part of our wiring and in the oldest regions of the brain, the amygdala and limbic system. To stay alert, constantly shifting focus, letting our mind pass over random thoughts and things like a monkey swinging through trees is natural but also very undisciplined.

I like to think of the mind like a faithful dog. Like your beloved pet, it's good to let it run. But it's also good to give it some training and teach it focus. When you do, you will have a happier brain and be a happier you.

Why Do Hard Things?

Why do hard things? Because whether we realize it or not, we crave them deep down, and this activity can literally affect our DNA. A study was conducted in which people were given the choice between experiencing boredom or receiving a painful electric shock; 70% chose the shock. We feel more alive when doing, and achieving something difficult is what makes life interesting and worth living. If that's not enough to make you want to go out and do something hard, then consider that you might also live longer. When I said it's part of your DNA, I wasn't kidding. According to Dr. Sood, doing hard things affects the telomeres at the end of your chromosomes, and their length (and shortness) is related to your age. Impatience shortens those telomeres (or keeps them short). For that reason, feeling stress and being impatient can actually make you older, shortening your life.

By now you should be picking up on some ideas regarding your stressors and how to conquer hard things. What can you do to get more out of life and support an unthinking mind? Here are a few pieces of advice.

Embrace the Suck

This expression means to find something you like in the current thing you don't like. Many young people today have never been blessed with the teaching experience of long-term drudgery, servitude, apprenticeship, or conscription, and for that reason they are at a serious disadvantage. It's not their fault; they haven't been around much. They don't yet know what it's like to endure and conquer something with will, mental strength, and intestinal fortitude. Their mettle has never been tested and they don't know what they are capable of, how high they can go, or how much they can achieve. There are young people in my life who have not yet pursued these crucibles and sometimes advocate avoiding them altogether. I worry for them, that such experiences might be what separates them from greater fulfillment and a more enriching life.

Make a List of What You Don't Like

There's a lot of talk about finding out what you like but we often have no idea what that is, so we potentially set ourselves up for frustration and churn trying to find our happiness and purpose in others' opinions. This happens in part when we listen to the ill-informed opinions of our peers instead of acting on and following our own path, any path, doing independent research, and asking the opinions of those senior to us.

The idea is to get out there and act at the same time you're listening to your friend's suspect advice. There's a ton of polarized talk along the lines of exclusively pursuing the things you like, while rejecting and avoiding everything else. This is patently bad advice, whether it's given by society, pop culture, the uninformed, or some bitter relative, or whether you simply perceive it's a good idea to snub everything and do nothing until your purpose hits you on the head. To figure out what you want from life, start with a list of what you *know* you don't (not your friends' list) and then look for the opposite of those things.

Learn to Tolerate Discomfort

That simple advice from my survival school instructor is timeless. As the late Wayne Dyer said, "When you change the way you look at things, the things you look at change." Find some good in your current misery and change it to tolerance. Thanks to mirror neurons in the brain, we mimic each other's behavior and catch others' moods. Others are constantly looking to you for signs regarding how they might feel. So if you're looking for a reason to keep a positive face in a lousy situation, practice some leadership and do it for the others around you.

Build Routine and Structure

Many people today think that freedom shouldn't require things like repetition, routine, structure, effort, or hard work. But the truth is there's no quicker way to get yourself enslaved to someone or something, and miserable, than to do nothing and give your power and control away. Freedom is achieved from the inside. There is freedom in discipline, in strength, in structure, even suffering. While I'm not telling you to go out and flog yourself, I am saying to not avoid difficulty when it visits; instead, use it. Even the most successful creative, unstructured, undisciplined, and independent person put effort and hard work into their bliss. To them, the structures they leveraged and endured weren't cages, but vehicles in which to fly. Confidence is the affirmation of a healthy structure and an important waystation on the road to your hero's story.

Recently I read a list of things confident people won't do written by Dr. Travis Bradberry. Confidence, Bradberry said, is different from egotistical swagger, which involves bravado. Here is an excerpt from Bradberry's post (https://www.talentsmarteq.com/articles/10-Things-Confident-People-Dont-Do/):

"1. **They don't make excuses.** If there's one trait confident people have in spades, it's self-efficacy. . . It's about having an internal locus of control rather than an external one.

"2. **They don't quit.** Confident people see both problems and failures as obstacles to overcome rather than impenetrable barriers to success.

"3. **They don't wait for permission to act.** Confident people don't need somebody to tell them what to do or when to do it. They see what needs to be done, and they do it.

"4. **They don't seek attention.** Confident people are masters of attention diffusion. When they're receiving attention for an accomplishment, they quickly shift the focus to all the people who worked hard to help get them there.

"5. **They don't need constant praise.** Confident people don't think that their success is dependent on other people's approval, and they understand that no matter how well they perform, there's always going to be somebody out there offering nothing but criticism.

"6. They don't put things off. Because they believe in themselves and expect that their actions will lead them closer to their goals, they don't sit around waiting for the right time or the perfect circumstances.

"7. They don't pass judgment. Confident people know that everyone has something to offer, and they don't need to take other people down a notch to feel good about themselves.

"8. They don't avoid conflict. Confident people see conflict as something to manage effectively. They know that conflict is part of life and that they can't avoid it without cheating themselves out of the good stuff, too.

"9. They don't let a lack of resources get in their way. Confident people don't get thrown off course just because they don't have the right title, the right staff, or the money to make things happen.

"10. They don't get too comfortable. Confident people understand that getting too comfortable is the mortal enemy of achieving their goals. They understand that a little discomfort is sometimes a good thing.

No Regrets

Editor Diana Bruk said the biggest regret people have in life is not the things they do but instead the things they *don't* do. Our sense of self can be broken into three categories: our "actual self," consisting of qualities we believe we possess; our "ideal self," made up of qualities we want; and our "ought self," the person we feel we should be according to obligations, responsibilities, and societal pressure. Researchers found that, when asked to name their single biggest life regret, 76% said it was not fulfilling their *ideal self*. We live in a world in which we're told we'll have a great life if we follow the rules. But those are behaviors associated with the *ought self*. When it comes to your dreams and aspirations, people are more likely to let them go unrealized, and that's what stings most later in life.

When we evaluate our lives, we do so in terms of achieving our "ideal" selves, becoming who we want to be. If we're not actively devoting time to pursuing this, those will be the regrets that stick, because we will look at them through the windshield of life. Irene Blecker, Rosenfeld Professor at Cornell, said it's not normal to put off your hopes and dreams indefinitely. "Short term, people regret their actions more than inactions, but long term, the inaction regrets stick around longer." Get out there and do something hard!

Doing Hard Things:
The Hero Comes Home

It was around 2012 and I was working as a program analyst. I was a guy in a cubicle. I had a 12-mile commute to a neighboring city where I spent most days sitting at my desk, doing data processing, and building PowerPoint presentations someone else would give. It was mostly boring work. During that same time, my son was spending summers and holidays at home between college semesters hoping to make extra money and had gotten a job as a junior analyst with a large consulting firm in the same town. For two summers and a couple Christmas and Easter breaks, we commuted together, and he got to experience what my daily life had been like for some 5 years. My son didn't offer much in the way of his feelings about his job during that time. Most mornings he slept as I drove and, in the afternoons, he impatiently texted me, "Are you here yet?"

I didn't think he took much from the experience and it wasn't until years later that he confessed to me there was little he liked about those days. Early wake ups, Excel spreadsheets, PowerPoint presentations and Word documents, arbitrary deadlines, meetings and more meetings, neckties, and suits—it felt like a repetitive, stressful, and constraining grind. But when he made that confession to me, he also added a revelation: It was the best professional work training he'd ever received, and he drew from it daily in his current job. During difficult times as the manager of a software company, that professional tempering was one of the secrets of his success.

In the last chapter we discussed embracing the suck, learning to tolerate discomfort, and living our own hero story. This chapter continues the conversation by drilling down into the commonalities of mankind, those things that have been with us for an eternity and will continue to challenge us. If we can find common patterns along these oddly familiar yet different paths, and if we can agree upon paths all of us follow, then perhaps we can not only plan a hero's journey for a lifetime but also map a way back to our beginning by the end of it.

If I were to implant a "foot stomp" at this point to get your attention, perhaps it would be to make the point that often we consciously work too hard in attempts to affect and predict the future, to find our purpose and discover "it," ultimately forcing unnatural and unfavorable imbalances and outcomes from the universe. The balance I'm suggesting is like that of riding a wave. It's a balance between what you want and what the universe wants of you. Maybe it's a balance between what our conscious mind thinks it wants and what our subconscious mind hides inside and feels it needs. Maybe it's even a "duality/triality" balance—the *conscious* and *subconscious mind*, and the *universe* we continually bump into and around in. We have no control of the trajectory of the expanding universe's wave and time's arrow. We can consciously catch it and ride it, but even in this we have no choice. As we consciously decide how to ride the wave, it's the subconscious mind, the unthinking mind, that masters the energy of the universe's wave. To use the surfing analogy again, if this were an exercise of the conscious rational mind, we would wipe out every time.

Adjusting to "Hard"

The reality of "hard" is a subjective thing, and that's due not to the physical reality of the hardness of things but instead to the internal reality of our mind's perception of hard. One could convincingly argue that scaling a mountain peak or earning a college degree is infinitely harder than traversing a parking lot, filling out a job application for a fast-food restaurant, or completing kindergarten, but you'd be wrong in assuming this and would be doing those around you a disservice. Part of adjusting to hard is to admit that the degree of difficulty is in part a perception that originates in the mind. When you do this, "hard" disappears and is replaced with curiosity, and with it disappears the thoughts and memories that had bounded its original description.

Physicist David Bohm said memory clutters the mind and our thought is never equal to the whole of something. It is a *representation*, an incomplete "re-presentation" of what was seen or felt. Yet we are ready to accept our thoughts as complete descriptions of what is, reality, when they're more like limited facsimiles.

Power vs Force

You can change your behavior for an easier life and one that is more enjoyable and fulfilling. A colleague recently reacquainted me with the work of David Hawkins, MD, PhD and his 2012 book *Power vs. Force*. His *map of consciousness* chart can best be described as a *consciousness maturity model* that is calibrated to attributes. Using the concept of calibration to express maturity, Hawkins contends that many people calibrate around 250 or lower, with fewer and fewer people at the higher levels of the scale.

Force:
- Scale (log of), 20: Shame. Emotion of humiliation.
- Scale, 30: Guilt. Emotion of blame.
- Scale, 50: Apathy. Emotion of despire.
- Scale, 75: Grief. Emotion of regret.
- Scale, 100: Fear. Emotion of anxiety.
- Scale, 125: Desire. Emotion of craving.
- Scale, 150: Anger. Emotion of hate.
- Scale, 175: Pride. Emotion of dignity (scorn).

Power:
- Scale, 200: Courage. Emotion of affirmation.
- Scale, 250: Neutrality. Emotion of trust.
- Scale, 310: Willingness. Emotion of optimism.
- Scale, 350: Acceptance. Emotion of forgiveness.
- Scale, 400: Reason. Emotion of understanding.
- Scale, 500: Love. Emotion of reverence.
- Scale, 540: Joy. Emotion of serenity.
- Scale, 600: Peace. Emotion of bliss.
- Scale, 700–1000: Enlightenment. Emotion of ineffable.

Hawkins' chart is a way to see where people are in terms of how they think about things, with self-interest being the lowest and enlightenment and spiritual pursuits being the highest. This maturity model forces individuals to admit where they are on the scale and where they need to improve. A value below 200 represents life-draining energy, and a value above 200 represents life-supporting energy. People on lower levels are more apt to use force to get their way, i.e., to bully, beguile, or push people around to get results. Power, on the other hand, is about inspiring, enlightening, and connecting so people go along willingly.

This scale also speaks to emotional intelligence. At scores of 175 and below, individuals do not have the courage to stand up and do the right thing and have too much pride to admit they have done something wrong. They also experience anger, insecurity, and fear of those who are different. People at lower levels also tend to default to basic human desires and blame others for problems, never accepting responsibility. In contrast, consider the people whom humanity would perceive as achieving higher calibration rankings such as Jesus, Muhammad, Mother Teresa, Gandhi, Confucius, the Dalai Lama, Krishna, Zoroaster, the pope, and others throughout history. Also, those who meditate regularly are shown to have higher rankings on Hawkins' scale, as they have calmed their minds, tap into their intuitive subconscious, and connect with a larger world.

Hawkins contends that as humans evolve, the numbers of people who occupy the upper levels increases, and we will start to see more harmony with all things. Today we don't do much to raise our levels of consciousness, but some dedicate their lives to it, and they have seen the world differently. Jesus saw the world very differently than just about everyone else around him 2000 years ago. I wonder how we might see the world in another 2000 years.

Looking for Leaders

Before looking for leaders to help you through "hard," find and refine the leader in yourself and enlist their help. After that, any subsequent leaders you identify will be your equals and collaborators in the struggle and not icons or deities to hold at a distance.

Leadership is an endless hot topic and is often looked upon as a magic bullet. As we see it, if we could just get it right, the tumblers would turn to the correct combination of behaviors and actions, and everything would go brilliantly from then on. However, one of the reasons why we can't catch illusive leadership is because we are looking in the wrong places for something that is frequently right in front of us. We blindly overlook everyday acts of leadership and greatness with expectations of grandeur and spectacle. If leadership doesn't "wow" and shock us, it's not leadership. We additionally expect that someone will ceremoniously "herald in" leaders and their behavior; we've been programmed to expect these things.

A book written several years ago said there were currently 1500 definitions of leadership and 30 concepts. That number of definitions suggests two things. First, since leadership happens and work gets done, one of these definitions must be the correct one. Second, perhaps we constantly miss it because were thinking of it in the wrong sorts of ways, looking for it in the wrong places, and waiting for formal structures or institutions to announce it. Perhaps leadership has less to do with force and control and more to do with strength and support. Maybe it's not meant to be characterized as a bounded, tangible, or even a physical thing. Perhaps it's simply an ongoing byproduct of intention, effort, and support done well.

Ideas like these might shake traditional paradigms because they suggest a leaderless management model that is more transitory and shared than many could understand or be comfortable with. Besides that, if such an idea were to catch on, it might threaten a multimillion-dollar industry in leadership books, lectures, and training. This may have never have occurred to you, but sometimes the leadership moment belongs to you. When it does, use it.

Losing Your Way

Some heroes don't make it home. Perhaps this single thought troubles me most. Some get lost and cannot find their way back to the beginning. I think this may have happened to my grandmother and fear it may also be happening to someone I think of as my sister. A friend recently asked me a popular question of our time: What happens to those who don't pursue their passions? Have they lost their way? Conversely, I would ask: What happens to someone who did nothing but pursue theirs? Could they also get lost? My answer to both those questions is yes. Many people today think freedom shouldn't require things like repetition, routine, structure, effort, pain, hard work, or even servitude, but the truth is there's no quicker way to get yourself enslaved to someone or something, and miserable, than to do nothing and give your power and control away. Freedom is an inside job and not necessarily a reflection of your outside predicament.

I think becoming lost is caused in part by an imbalanced life. Ignoring and not pursuing one's passion is a common theme often cited as cause of an unfulfilled, unrealized life, but so is doing nothing but following one's passion. Life is part divergence and part convergence; part exploration and part exploitation; part pushing the gas pedal to the floor and climbing and part letting off the gas and coasting downhill; part maverick independence and autonomy and part service to others, selflessness, and paying dues. If we are doing life right, we reap and we sow, and we ebb and we flow. Some never stop and shift position, exercising all of life's patterns, and they spend a lifetime out of balance until the end.

What do I mean when I talk about finding our way back home? Earlier, I discussed a "meta-reality." It's a reality beyond our everyday world, a truer reality above the one in which we live, with all that has defined us and all we have accumulated stripped away. Opinions, circumstances, and actions define, bound, and border who we have become. Our true meta-reality is the original clear spring we originated from vs the muddy delta we have become after years of living. If we could strip away the vegetation, wash away the dirt, filter out the sediment, and remove the distractions, we would see more clearly what we are at our core from that original stream. Finding our way back home is a journey back to our original selves. Clearing a path for the unthinking intuitive mind to join us in our conscious efforts navigating this journey is our goal.

A Humanity Thing

In the last section on doing hard things, I had a section called "Embrace the Suck," where I commented that young people were avoiding hard things. When I originally posted this section online, it generated great conversation, and some thoughtful critiques.

One of those critiques was from my son. He and his spouse are lifetime learners and have their own outdoor adventure company and coaching business. After buying their first home and settling down in Pittsburgh, they did something unconventional. They sold their house, converted a retired paramedic ambulance into a tiny home, and began traveling the country, spending half of their time on the East Coast and half on the West Coast.

My son's critique was that I "missed the mark" regarding today's young. Their struggle, he said, was not in avoiding the difficult but instead in deciding which difficulties to invest in while defining and determining the value of achievement. He added that *"achievement for achievement's sake was likely an exercise in distraction."*

While on one level he's right, we mustn't waste precious time engaged in trivial or unproductive pursuits. I would also argue that it's all "grist for the mill"; even an un-useful experience that currently seems wasteful actually may not be later. How do we know in the moment?

Potentially, everything and anything that happens or presents itself to us has the potential to help us grow, to support us, and to better us. It all depends on our processing of and perspective on each experience. If one were to consciously, exclusively "pick and choose" what experiences to accept in life, this would be an exercise of the conscious mind; it wouldn't allow the conscious or sub-conscious to be confronted by an unexpected experience and would steer us towards a one-sided life perspective. There's a part of nature that cannot be harnessed, controlled, predicted, planned, or deferred, though it's our nature to try and manipulate it.

A reluctance to launch, or commit, has plagued humanity for time immemorial. What's the solution? My thoughtful son and daughter-in-law already have the answers. He said they are pursuing a thorough understanding of what success means to them, and that will guide their next move. That's a great outlook. If everyone took such a methodical and researched approach to life, the world would be a very different and less chaotic place. Seeking to better understand, I looked up the definition of *achievement*. It means accomplishment, by ability, effort, courage, or deed. The practice and betterment of life using such nouns in the pursuit of achievement (for achievement's sake) seems worthwhile to me and only useless distraction if nothing is learned from it.

Questions like these are not a "you or me," or "us and them" thing; rather, they're a humanity thing. Understand that your experiences, while unique to you, are also a variation on shared human themes which repeat, and they're iterative. In a literal sense, "blazing your own trail" is an impossibility. It's inevitable that your next move has been done before in some fashion by someone else; the only difference is you. What were their experiences and feelings? If you are reluctant to make your next move from presented choices because they're not on your schedule, overcome that fear. See what's been done before, take the first step, and then see what happens.

I'm reminded of a wonderfully ridiculous Jim Carrey movie in which he went to a motivational seminar and began to say yes to everything. Life should be more like this, only maybe not to Carrey's extreme. Famous biologist Robert Sapolsky in a popular Stanford University lecture on human behavioral biology, complexity, and emergence said something relevant to this discussion. He said that when considering things like biologically cellular starting states in nature, mature end states, and cell patterns that mature into living organisms, "you cannot look at the mature state and tell what the starting state pattern was." Conversely, he says, "Considering starting states gives you no indication of what the mature state will look like."

So what's the answer as to the proper conducting of a life? Mix it up, plan some things, and trip into and discover others. Commit to all of it, even if it's initially only in your thoughts, and leave room for and pay attention to what might emerge and consider those who have previously walked similar paths. As for my son and daughter-in-law's tiny home adventure, in 1993 my wife and I bought a late model 30-foot class A motor home and spent 3 months driving it from Alaska to Florida. It was quite an adventure.

Heroes Discover Their Own Journey

Another thoughtful commentary came from Carmel Finnan, a storytelling strategist and marketing mentor based in Berlin. Carmel reminded me with her story that the challenges faced by the young are not only an American thing, but they're also a humanity thing. Carmel said, "The hero comes home when they discover their unique journey in their own way." She indicated that a great deal of our lives is wasted trying to fit into a mold made for someone else and by someone else. Carmel said she has a son who has always challenged her 'conventional' views. One thing she attested to regarding young people is that they have their own journey to find what matters to them and then pursue it. It's not like our journey. While some themes persist in life, others have changed.

Carmel said today's youth are children of an age of technology, a digital economy age some have dubbed the fourth industrial revolution, which includes artificial intelligence, machine learning, robotics, and nanotechnology. This new age is challenging our lives in unprecedented ways and challenging our young to reimagine fundamental things in life such as the workplace, free time, relationships, and health. Carmel said she doesn't think we realize what is happening in the world today. Our young will face their challenges in a different way, or they won't face them and that will have consequences, as it did with us. Young people will live their hero's journey by walking through it as we had to do. As biologist Robert Sapolsky said, "You can't predict it, you must march through it." Our hero's task as elders is to allow them the space to do it, the encouragement, and the understanding.

Carmel was also concerned about what happens to those who don't pursue their passions. She wanted to know how they let those chances slip away and whether they had regrets. What are the signals we ignore about following our dreams? As a former educator in Germany, the system suited 70% or 80% of the population but lost 20% to 30%. The latter ended up lost unless they had the luck or tenacity to find their true talents and pursue them.

For this group, the hero's journey was not a conventional one. Some who failed in traditional settings later became the inventors and creatives who shaped our era. In a great RSA Animate video, Sir Ken Robinson outlined what Carmel referred to. Our global educational paradigms need to change and be revised for the 21st century.

Personally, Carmel said she didn't know she wasn't living her purpose for a long time. She fit the mold of her family, though it was never a life that suited her. It took her a long time to understand that conventional pathways were not the ones she wanted to walk. Carmel said we must learn to listen to our voice, then as parents, teachers, and mentors, learn to listen to the voice of those who haven't yet found their way.

Beyond Hard

In his book *Can't Hurt Me, Master Your Mind and Defy the Odds*, David Goggins said that what matters most in life is work ethic. He said our society has become addicted to "quick fixes," but only hard work leads to success. David should know. Growing up in an abusive household, he suffered traumatic stress to such a degree it caused him to have a severe learning disability and gain a dangerous amount of weight. By early adulthood he was functionally illiterate and approaching 300 pounds.

What kinds of things did David do to move past his potentially crippling childhood and make the best of each moment? One thing was to get up early. In addition to working hard, David advises people to "win the morning." He started every day at 4 am with a 10-mile run before putting in 8 to 9 hours in the office. He also said to "do one hard thing each day." David became one of the U.S. Navy's few African American Navy Seals and in 2006, he completed the Badwater 9000, an ultramarathon considered to be the "world's toughest foot race." A 135-mile endurance race covering 9,000 feet in elevation changes, it starts in Death Valley, California, in July and ends at 8,000 feet at the base of Mount Whitney. If David can endure such hardship, make such positive changes, and achieve such goals, what can you do?

Clearheaded

The universe is order, humanity is chaos, and our minds lie in the balance. What does it mean to have a clear head? It means a great deal more than you might think and is harder to achieve than you might imagine, perhaps even impossible. If we can clear our minds and gain control of them, we could see our hero's path from our origins, and our way back to the beginning clearly. Freeing the unthinking intuitive mind to play its part is the way. There's an old saying that on a clear day, you can see forever. Unfortunately, humanity has had few truly clear days; it's just the way we're wired.

So why is humanity so chaotic, and what's it doing to us? There are many reasons, to include dualistic thinking, thinking of ourselves and others as both subject and object; an ego identity that identifies itself in terms of thoughts and things; embracing a mechanistic model to explain life; self-deceptive thoughts and trying to keep our busy minds distracted. What it's doing to us could be even worse, heralding our impending extinction.

Self-Deception and the Cluttered Mind

Part of our problem has to do with our thoughts that are a jumbled mess of emotions, fear, bias, and self-deception, restricting clear thinking. Human thought is the chief reason for our disorder. But why is human thought so disorderly? According to spiritualist J. Krishnamurti and physicist David Bohm, it's due to self-deceptive thinking, which comprises most of man's thinking without us being aware of it. Chief antagonist of our mental limitations is *desire*, they attest, which leads to self-deception. Bohm said that most of man's thoughts are self-deceptive and are tailored to rationalize what we do and what we want. In life, we naturally have desires, and Bohm said we create self-deceptions to justify the objects we crave (the objects of our desire). Eventually, this thoughtless pursuit of things, this self-deception, leads to incoherence and irrationality.

Bohm stated that what we are really searching for in the pursuit of desire is a state of perfection, comfort, and safety. We are really seeking a connection with our authentic selves. We have also allowed thought to become our ruler but thought with all its limitations and fallacies should only participate in our life, not rule it. Thought is an abstraction of reality, a limited representation and not a complete picture. Thought, which is built on language and words with all its descriptive richness, can still be painfully limited in accurately expressing everything that is going on and that the body and senses perceives. Bohm says the minute the mind attaches itself to something—a thought, an action, a deed, an idea—a kind of corruption begins, a bias toward that thought. Your mind becomes connected to the thing it has attached itself to, and this inhibits original thought, new ideas, and creativity. No matter how independently you may believe you're acting or thinking, those actions and thoughts are founded on and linked to their predecessors.

A second reason we can't think clearly is because we can't get thoughts out of our heads and clear our minds. Our minds are always full. Bohm and Krishnamurti both said that thinking clearly requires "unrestricted attentiveness," which means clearing our minds of everything and embracing nothing, a truly terrifying notion for humanity. Even during leisure time, our minds are filled with distraction. The original Greek meaning of the word *leisure* meant "empty space," but now, every space is filled with structure, activity, distraction, and things. Every minute of our day, every aspect of society, and every facet of our minds is occupied with something, whether we are at rest or at work.

Perhaps the most terrifying of all of man's fears, the idea of emptiness, or nothingness, doesn't sit right with humanity and strikes fear because it represents loss, the loss of our very existence. To "have nothing" or "be nothing" is a condition we avoid for a lifetime. In our language and in society, "nothing" literally suggests to us that we may not exist. The Latin root for the word *real* means "thing" and "to think." So real means "all things," or things which the mind can think about. *Nothing* can mean empty space (a void), or worthlessness, or it can mean "no-thing" as in nothing physical and therefore nothing real, no life.

There's a terror in removing the (physical) things in our lives on which we think our existence depends. They bound our reality and validate our existence. Physical "things" create a psychological security that is tangible. Nonphysical thought alone cannot provide this comfort for humanity, at least not yet. With 188 known cognitive biases, prerecorded tapes in the mind written long ago, prejudices, and social conditioning, it's a wonder any of us are truly aware of anything around us and that new thoughts even get into our psyche.

How can this knowledge help you write your unique hero's story and find your way home? By simply reading this, and knowing some of these traps and pitfalls, you have already been helped. When you begin to see the disorder in thought, it will begin to fall away. What is the intelligence beyond thought? Beyond thought, there is *awareness* and *observation*; these are also features in the unthinking mind. When you start to move past a preoccupation with everyday thoughts and into these overlooked higher levels of intelligence, you will feel yourself beginning to change.

The Arc of Life

I would love to find for you the formula, the magical combination, so that every aspect of your life would suddenly "click" into place. However, I can't do that. Besides, what fun would that be? Conflict and contrast give meaning to life, right? Could we live in a world without conflict? Could we live with ourselves without it? Maybe, if I can't provide a magic pill, I can at least set you on a better path. Perhaps one of the secrets is that life is like an arc, or a bell curve characterizing attributes, abilities, and the experience of life. In the provided diagram, we move from low to high and back to low again in one of the depicted curves, and move in the opposite direction (high-low-high) in the other. The two arcs shown are dichotomies to represent life's journey: when one is high, the other is low.

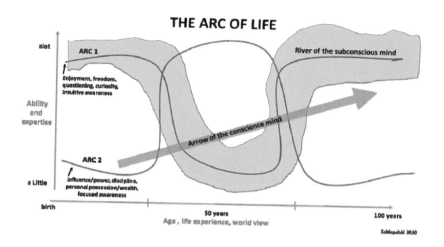

THE ARC OF LIFE

a lot

ARC 1

River of the subconscious mind

Enjoyment, freedom,
questioning, curiosity,
intuitive awareness

Ability
and
expertise

Arrow of the conscience mind

ARC 2

a Little

influence/power, discipline,
personal possession/wealth,
focused awareness

birth

50 years

100 years

Age, life experience, world view

Zehlapahbi 2020

Which attributes and abilities are better for the whole of our lives by the end? What should you possess "a little of" or "a lot of" in order to say you have lived successfully? If this diagram has merit, then our challenge might be to find a "middle path" and balance upon the two as we ride those waves from beginning to end.

"We Can Do This the Easy Way or the Hard Way"

There are lots of good reasons to get the *hard* in life out of the way first. You have more mental and physical stamina when you're young; it builds confidence and introduces familiarity; and when you get these processes into your muscle memory, they will serve you well later when you need them. The late spiritualist J. Krishnamurti said, "Life is relationships and actions." Focus your attention and efforts on these things and everything else will figure itself out.

While reading an annual birthday message from the Commandant of the U.S. Marine Corps to his troops, General Berger shared a quote from an American novelist that seems appropriate to our discussion about living your unique hero story:

> "In times of change and danger when there is quicksand of fear under men's reasoning, a sense of continuity with generations gone before can stretch like a lifeline across the scary present"
> —John Dos Passos

157

Proprioception of Thought and Unthinking

A while back, I said human thought was the chief reason for humanity's problems. I'm more convinced of this now than ever before. If we could learn to corral and harness our thought, we would lead much more contented lives, and probably solve the planet's woes. If we could do this collectively as a species, it could change the world.

I don't mean to say that "thinking" is a problem that needs to be eradicated. On the contrary, it can be very valuable. Rather, I'm saying that the ways in which we *use* and *think* about thought are fundamentally wrong. We don't have a good grasp on what's going on in the continual thought bubbles floating over our heads, nor do we know how to use thought properly. Additionally, I suspect that our minds are capable of much more rationality, computing power, art, beauty, and connectivity than we currently use them for, but we have yet to discover how to use them. At present, we're cognitively not much more than chickens scratching the dirt for seeds.

As it currently stands and probably has for a mega-annum (a million years), our thoughts rule the roost over our perception and run roughshod over everything we do—most of the time messing up perfectly good decision making with dubious advice you wouldn't take from your best friend. We give conscious thought too much of a pass, never questioning its counsel as if it's ethereal and otherworldly. And we too often give it the last word when it should be part of a collected data set to help us determine the best course of action. What's worse is that when the conscious mind does reach back to the subconscious to help navigate its world, which surprisingly is 80% to 90% of our waking day, it's only to replay prerecorded tapes from its memory, not to channel the vast connection to the implicate order, draw from intuition and gut feeling, or draw from the wisdom of the unthinking mind. No

158

longer can we let our busy inner dialogue of conscious thought exclusively steer the bus, because it's driving us toward a perilous cliff endangering humanity, chaining us to reflexive incoherent behavior, clouding and wasting our precious lives.

Proprioception is a word originally from occupational therapy I wasn't familiar with. It was introduced to me by the late physicist David Bohm and has been called the sixth sense. What follows is my interpretation of the works of Bohm on his ideas of *proprioception of thought*, which were presented in a series of weekend lectures given in 1990 in Ojai, California.

What Is Proprioception?

Pronounced proh-pree-*uh*-sep-shuhn, the term means *self-perception* or *self-awareness* and traditionally has to do with the physiology of the body. Literally meaning *governed by proprioceptors*, it concerns awareness of the position of one's body in space. A proprioceptor is a receptor located in our muscles and tendons that responds to stimuli produced within the body. Think of it as being aware of what your body is doing without having to be consciously aware. When you're sitting in a chair, you're aware of sitting in a chair and can unconsciously maintain this position; with it, you won't slither off onto the floor. If you're reaching for something, you are aware your arm and hand are doing that and where they are moving in space. Keep in mind that if we didn't have proprioception of the body, we would be nonviable; we wouldn't survive.

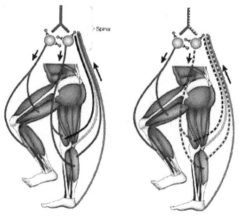

What Is Proprioception of Thought?

What lies beyond thought? As proposed by David Bohm, it's *proprioception of thought*. There is an intelligence beyond thought—one that should be in the driver's seat of our lives but is instead relegated to the back. This intelligence is *awareness* and *observation*. Bohm suggested that awareness and observation check in before thought, advising and informing it, and this triad of awareness, observation, and thought should create *perception*. However, Bohm said that thought hijacks this process, creating a narrative first. It paints a picture presenting an abstract reality of what's happening, rationalizing, and modifying awareness and observation to fit its model instead of using its feedback, when in fact observation and awareness saw it first and more accurately. The result? We either come away with a feeling that thought is wrong or a thought that feeling is wrong but are not sure which.

The chief problem with thought being at the helm, solely running this process, is that it's too biased and preoccupied with things like self-identity protection, the physical material world, memory, and other stuff to solely render an objective opinion of reality. It can't coherently perform this task without the input of awareness and observation and a self-awareness of its own limitations. As Bohm saw it, thought, albeit subtle, is a muscle reflex, physical, neurochemical, and material. When thought exclusively creates the story first, crowding out awareness and observation, the abstraction it creates is taken from memory and not the present. This is a problem. The idea that we have elevated thought to a divine level of clairvoyance is doing us, and humanity, a grave disservice and endangering us as a species.

Awareness and Observation

Before thought there is awareness and observation. Think of them as components of feelings. The process sounds simple: get the order right and you have clear "self-awareness of thought" (proprioception) but get it wrong and it's a different story. Thoughts often show up at the same time as awareness and observation, and the three fire off inputs simultaneously. Unless we sort and classify our thoughts with these feelings, they quickly get confused and jumbled.

Part of the problem is that most thoughts are memories of experience, awareness, and observation and may not be related to current awareness and observation, particularly if they come before the current awareness and observation. However, thought would lead you to believe it is *always* connected to the present situation and not to judgments, bias, memories, or physical and neuro-chemical repeating reflexive actions. In its defense, it's not entirely thought's fault. Thought may honestly believe this new situation is the same as every previous one; after all, thought is a muscle reflex of the mind.

Correct proprioception of thought, then, is awareness + observation + thought—and *self-perception*, or *self-awareness* of thought, is a coalescence of these three.

We've established that human thought is a muscle reflex and should probably, respectfully, be relegated to the status of a burp of gas bubbles or a knee-jerk. It might serve you better to think of thought as a slow reflexive knee jerk, often too slow to make a connection to perception, and too pronounced, frequent, and vocal to ignore. Because of this lag between thought, feeling, and reaction, you may not realize it came from you. Like any other muscle reflex in the body, thoughts condition themselves to repeat, and if they produce comforting feel-good endorphins, their likelihood of repeating increases dramatically.

How do we know thought hasn't manipulated our feelings, awareness, and observation? Any feeling not produced by thought is part of our perception. However, thought will try to convince you proprioception isn't necessary, that it can handle everything on its own. The view that thought is telling you everything you need to know, the way things are, and that awareness and observation aren't necessary has been conditioned into it as a repeating reflex.

David Bohm shared an ancient saying about identity from an unknown author: "*I don't know what I am. What I am is unknown but constantly revealing itself.*"

Based on these ideas, you can question your thoughts and make sure they're connected to right here, right now. Next, work on sharpening awareness and observation; they're the gateway to your feelings. Ask questions of thought based on the cues they're providing instead of advocating their feelings and then letting your mind paint its own comfortable reflexive narrative. Finally, search for truth and share your thoughts. When we share thoughts, they're more likely to be coherent, bringing us closer to truth. Sharing gives thought the benefit of comparison, and we achieve a higher level of consciousness because meaning happens between us. Bohm said that "truth is a perception and then an action." Thought alone is not perception, and it's not truth. It's a reflex caused by something else. If thought is your only guiding action throughout life, it is incoherent action ill informed. Get these things right, and you will connect the thinking mind with the intuitive wisdom of the unthinking mind.

Proprioception in Companies

What would it mean if a company had great self-awareness, great self-perception, and proprioception? It would have the ultimate culture—culture nirvana! It would also have a learning culture, with minimal incoherence and contradictions, and it would be ambidextrous. Successful companies breathe in and out like living organisms, continuously renewing and refreshing themselves (with negative entropy). *Movement* is good because a static organization is likely a dead or dying one. Exploration and exploitation (ambidexterity) have more to do with surfing an optimal edge of a wave between chaos and calm than it does with trying to operate in a balanced static state. Ambidexterity is a model, designed to be used in motion. Traditional organizational models, while they feel comfortable, appear sensible, and look idyllic, are usually just snapshots in time.

Knowing

"The intuitive mind is a sacred gift, and the rational mind is a faithful servant. We have created a society that honors the servant and has forgotten the gift." —Albert Einstein

Do you remember the quote from the popular National Lampoon movie *Animal House*? "Fat, drunk, and stupid is no way to go through life." In that spirit, the brain has flaws. It's fiercely faithful, but also chronically lazy and frequently wrong. We need to praise it for tirelessly trying to protect us, for looking for energy-saving short cuts and providing comfortingly familiar paths of thought to safely walk us down, but we shouldn't let it get lazy or jaded, because it will. And we shouldn't assume it knows everything. Instead, we need to give it new growth-stretching challenges and experiences. You know what's best for your brain, not the other way around. Also, don't let it rob you of your cognitive sobriety by inebriating and enticing your incorrigible ego with thoughts of grandeur and perfection. We are always works in progress, never finished products.

What *is* enough to bolster thought and our brain and what should we do? Frequently question thought's opinion by checking it against other cues. This chapter discusses why thought alone is not enough for humanity to live by. It delves deeper into thought and truth and looks at how to tell when we're on the best cognitively proprioceptive path, not only for our own benefit and to encourage more "unthinking" moments, but for the benefit of all humankind.

Knowledge and Knowing

There's a subtle yet important distinction between *knowledge* and *knowing*, and not recognizing this distinction hurts us. It's so important, in fact, that not knowing this difference most likely robs us of learning and growing, keeping us skipping like a scratched 78 RPM record at the same point in the song. Now, consider that we are social animals and mirror neurons in our brain cause us to imitate one other. My skipping song is likely to be heard, and even hummed, by you and others, in families, communities, cultures, even countries. Its influence is deeper and more far reaching than we know. Such a result paints a sad epitaph not only for an un-realized life, but even for an unrealized species. We are affected by, and mimic, one another.

Neuroscientist and Harvard professor Rudy Tanzi said you should never explain your theories, especially if you're a student at Harvard. Tanzi said we are infinitely smarter in our heads than we are when we speak. Why? Even with 100 billion neurons firing in the brain, when we try to vocally reduce what we know to "laryngeal grunt sounds," we are limited, and we lose much of our brilliance in translation. It's not just that we don't know enough; it's also that we can't convey with words all that we perceive, nor definitively capture it in an ever-changing picture.

Tanzi conveyed what Bohm, Krishnamurti, Einstein, Chopra, Eckert Tolle, and countless other great thinkers through time also knew: knowledge (data, facts, and figures) is limited, but *knowing*, (learning) is limitless. If you're going to anchor on any single idea in life, this is a good one to pick. Even with this sage advice, we still stubbornly park on current and popular knowledge as the standard by which to measure, judge, act, and interact, instead of keeping our mind open, learning, and updating what we know against the ever-changing picture of our world.

What's the difference between *knowledge, knowing,* and *learning*? You might say one difference is "tense." Knowledge is in the past tense while "knowing" doesn't have a tense, or, if it does, it's an ever-receding future tense. The difference between knowledge and knowing is *learning*, which is neither static nor in the past, but is continually forward moving and forward thinking.

How do you make this quantum leap from knowledge to knowing? You start by putting thought in its proper (optimal) place within the rank and file of perception, and then you begin paying more attention to observation and awareness. Once you master this, you're home free and will find the unthinking mind accompanying the conscious mind through every experience.

I have a good friend, Rob Bogosian, who asks each of his MBA students the same question: "What's more important in your workplace, knowledge or learning?" Undoubtedly, they almost exclusively answer "knowledge." This view of having specific knowledge as more important than learning may represent the biggest mistake organization cultures make and one that keeps them from becoming learning organizations. It hobbles them, stops them cold. It's difficult to diagnose and correct, and the problems don't stop there.

Most of us crave definitive answers and knowledge and then transmogrify data, facts, and figures into our own identities. Knowledge becomes us and defines us. Unfortunately "shunning learning" scales easily and quickly among groups, organizations, and cultures. The bottom line is that the minute we plant a stake in the ground and defend knowledge, identifying with it and validating our existence by it, we lose.

Fantasy, Creativity, Imagination, and Perception

Fantasy, creativity, imagination, and perception are manifestations and expressions of thought and ultimately comprise part of perception. Though on the surface they may seem similar, they can be very different and are not necessarily interchangeable or mutually exclusive.

Perception

An "optimal perception," let's call it cognitive proprioception, can be defined as a kind of self-perception made of awareness, observation, and thought, with thought contributing to perception, giving it meaning. But it goes deeper than this. Unpacking these concepts further, it can be said that awareness, observation, and thought (perception) are heavily influenced by things like identity, ego, bias, and memory, which are brought in and transmitted by thought. This is also where imagination comes in. Imagination is a "re-imagining," or a re-creation of experience through our thoughts creating images and with them either pleasure or pain. These images are made up of reflexes in the mind drawn from memory, disturbing neurochemicals, and triggering neurons in the brain. In this way thoughts' imaginative speculations give rise to images and sensations, and we arrive at a continual seamless personal reality by which to navigate life.

Imagination

It can be said that everything we perceive as reality in our world is from the imagination. An "imaging" of what our brain filters through the senses and consciousness is created by this process. Bohm contended that imagination comprises everything from pedestrian day-to-day thoughts, images, and manifestations of reality (Bohm calls this primary imagination) to imaginings that are fanciful, abstract, and even brand new.

Fantasy and Creativity

Beyond the everyday imagination of rearranging, sorting, and interpreting reality, there are other types of imagination that represent a departure from daily reality. Things that are not necessarily real, may be known or unknown, and may be good, bad, or even dangerous to us are fantasy and creativity.

Fantasy, or fancy, Bohm said, is rooted in the past. You can fantasize about a tropical vacation or about new furniture in your living room. Either way, you are conjuring up images seen before, somewhere else in your past (from memory) or experiences previously had, heard, thought, or read about. Fantasy can be of great comfort and help or can become dangerous if it slips into everyday perception and merges with the daily filtering of the reality we experience and share with others. Imagination can be utilitarian, takes effort, and is helpful, or it can be destructive if it slips into fantasy, losing all connection to the real and the present.

Creativity, on the other hand, while being another form of imagination is not exclusively grounded in or tethered to memories and thought. It's more of an open and empty space, representing a placeholder for anything that might emerge to occupy it. Creativity, Bohm said, comes from somewhere else and allows our perception to draw from something other than conscious thought, memory, or reflex; it comes from somewhere deeper. Bohm said that consciousness is like a vast river, but the conscious part of our mind, daily reflexive thought, is little more than a ripple on the surface of this immense, deep river. Creativity occurs when we dive below the surface of consciousness and plunge into the subconscious and connect with something else we cannot reach in the conscious realm, seeing something new, and perhaps pulling it in from a larger connected universe. Creativity draws from the powers of the intuitive unthinking mind.

A Story of Connections

While doing some early morning writing for this chapter, I had my ear buds in, and a familiar song came on the radio. As I wrote, a thought suddenly came to my mind that my mother died on this very January day many years ago. It was not a thought I had intended to have or was even consciously thinking about. Full confession, I wasn't thinking about her and hadn't thought of her in quite some time. I noted the thought and as I continued writing, my thoughts went back to the lovely melody of the familiar song playing and an associated thought that my mother, also like me, liked this band, Chicago, and its upbeat music. Curious of the year of the song, I did a quick internet search, found the wiki and the album cover, which featured a cardinal, and discovered the song was written the year of her death, a curious coincidence.

A few moments later, my wife entered the room and asked what I was doing. I told her I was writing and shared the coincidence of thinking of Jeanne on this very day, and of the song and the album. Looking at my phone and the picture of the album I had found, she then exclaimed emphatically, "Look at the bird in the artwork of the album, that's a cardinal. Cardinals are an ancient symbol that departed loved ones are near!" I looked at her and the picture and unexpectedly I began to cry. This time (perhaps for the first time), they were tears of comfort and happiness I had never shed before. It's funny how thought, the human mind, perception and awareness, and the universe work. Was this very visceral transcendent experience a simple case of noticing, hyper-noticing, and sensemaking, or something more? You decide. Whatever the case, I do know the unthinking mind had a hand in creating that reality.

Moving Beyond Limitations of Thought

As discussed in the previous chapter, thoughts are representations of experience, ephemeral, transitory, and repeating. Thought is a muscle reflex of the brain not much different than a knee jerk or a flinch, and the brain is an organ that's like a muscle. And thought is also a matter of chemistry. Neurochemicals in the brain—dopamine, serotonin, and others—are released in response to outside stimuli and inside thought, and we respond in varying emotive reflexive ways.

Have you ever been inexplicably obsessed over something to the point that it became all consuming—young teenage love perhaps, or a new car—and then, just as quickly and mysteriously, it wasn't important to you any longer? You may have even thought "this thing is dead to me" when only a day earlier you were pining away desperately over that person or thing. That's an example of a brain being flooded with neurochemicals. However, despite this, there is something more to thought than chemicals, reflexes, firing neurons, and memory, something profound that we are only beginning to understand.

I have a yoga instructor friend in San Diego named Soraya who agrees that most thoughts are based on memories of past experience. She offered an additional perspective that further explains the struggle we have in living a truer, more healthy reality. Thoughts, Soraya said, are also based on projections of future experiences. While *awareness* and *observation* are deeply rooted in the present, thought isn't paying attention to that. Thought compulsively wants to ping-pong back and forth from memories of the past into projections of the future, also based on memory and future bets of what might be. Fueled by thoughts, emotions, and the anticipation of pleasure, pain, excitement, or fear, it's a troubling way to live, Soraya concludes.

Our mental, emotional, and physical health depend greatly upon cultivating an ability to live more and more in the present.

That means thought rooted in and informed by awareness and observation, making healthy and balanced use of both remembering the past and predicting the future. Soraya said there is so much more to us than our thinking minds. The trick is to step out of the compulsive back and forth of the past to future and discover the intelligence and ease of living in the present, informed by awareness and observation. That's proprioception, and unthinking.

With careful practice, we can achieve Bohm's proprioception of thought (self-awareness of thought), and humankind can step out of its past animal behavior, step around its mechanical model of humanity and rational present notions and future bets, and transcend into a yet conceivable future—one in which awareness, observation, and thought work together in perfect accord to bring us out of our isolated and fearful confusion, bring us true happiness and contentment, and welcome us into the light of a wonderfully connected universe that make all living things possible.

Identity and Coherence

Thoughts are like ripples on the surface of human consciousness. These reflexes create many representations (abstractions) of ourselves. They are all superficial compared to our consciousness. We don't know what the consciousness is made of, but we do know it's not as simple as parsing, segmenting, separating, and locking down consciousness as being "this" or "that." Bohm suggested that honestly trying to touch the self should be like trying to touch a rainbow: you will never get there; it will always recede as you approach it because it is ever changing. There is an ancient saying that the self, your essence, is unknown, ethereal, and constantly revealing itself, and everything that it creates and brings with it is part of that unknown revealing itself.

The I, the Me, and the Self

We can put our identity into, attach it, to anything: our body, our thoughts, our profession, our bank account, our stories of either heroism or victimhood. David Bohm asked, "Do we need an identity?" We can affix knowledge to our identities as well, although doing so is often dangerous and to our detriment. It has a polarizing, snapshot effect and suddenly we have to protect and defend that knowledge that defines us, it. Dr. Tanzi said, "Anything we pull into our consciousness ultimately comes back to govern, regulate, and monitor us," so consider what you're bringing into your consciousness.

The expression *me, myself, and I* originally comes from sociology and psychology as well as an old song from jazz/blues vocalist Billie Holiday. Our lives are often a confusing subject/object split because of the divisions we make between the *me*, how you think everyone else sees you, and the *I*, of the self, which is the authentic part of you. American sociologist Charles Cooley gave us the term "looking glass self," i.e., "how I see myself is a reflection of how you see me." In other words, I'm looking for my identity in your image of me. We see ourselves the way we think others see us.

The self develops with social experience, with symbols and identities. We put ourselves in others' shoes to try to see their intentions and to see how we like it. We also see ourselves the way we think society or culture sees us. Many roles and situations are derived from social interaction based on the two parts of self (I and me).

Sociologist George Meade and Cooley also talked about four stages of development: (1) infancy, with imitation and no sense of self-awareness; (2) play, in which the self takes on the role of one other person in one situation (one role, one situation); (3) games using rules; and (4) generalized other, with many roles and many situations. This becomes the maturity stage and culture becomes our looking glass, looking back at us.

Deception and Incoherence

There's a grievous problem with thought: it can be deceptive. Deception occurs with thought continuously, and if we could wrestle that single problem to the ground, we could eliminate 99% of humanity's problems. If we could collectively do this as a species, we could experience a heaven on earth.

No thought is entirely coherent because each is built on many variables—past memory, society and culture, ego and self-identity, bias, judgment, and of course awareness and observation. When we discover incoherence in our thought, we have two choices. Our attitude can either be to move toward coherence or to defend our incoherence. If something gives your brain feel good endorphins, even if it's wrong, you're likely to defend it. For the brain, it's all about feeling good, and for the ego it's all about protection and safety.

It's hard to define coherence beyond saying it is what's true, or just, or virtuous; coherence is largely contextual and situational. However, a good sign for incoherence is getting something (negative results) you don't intend, like conflict, stress, or confusion. But here is where it gets complicated. What if your coherence is incoherence? There are some who glory and delight in misery and destruction. They get feel-good endorphins from it and therefore will defend and protect unhealthy behavior. Sometimes even misery can be comforting and define our identity and satisfy our egos if we have internalized it and it has "become us." These people have built a second-order coherence to defend and justify their first-order incoherence, a kind of "incoherent coherence." Have you ever known anyone like that?

Because thought is like a muscle reflex, it wants to be sustained and repeat; that's what reflexes do, they continue. The only way to break incoherence is to break the muscle memory of it, stopping the reflexive action. This is an iterative process. The road to coherence is sometimes continued incoherence. It often takes time to kick a habit. Coherence, incoherence, perception, hunkering down on specific knowledge or the pursuit of truth and knowing, and the ego identity will also often come down to the environment and culture you exist in while you're experiencing it, and you may have little conscious awareness of it. Do you think a fish knows it's swimming in water?

What's the problem with someone else being an incoherent dolt and walking around unconscious? The answer is plenty. If we didn't have proprioception of the body, if we weren't aware of what our muscles and tendons were doing, we wouldn't survive. I fear that if we don't collectively develop a proprioception of thought, we will meet the same fate. Furthermore, unlike traditional physical proprioception, someone lacking proprioception of thought can give it to others easily.

One big promoter of incoherence today is technology. It keeps us diffused, distracted, and logging overtime in the left hemisphere of our brain and blocking or ignoring the intuitive unthinking insights that the right hemisphere of the mind brings. Psychiatrist Dr. Iain McGilchrist says that while the left hemisphere of the brain is chiefly concerned with apprehending things, the right is interested in comprehending them. Both are required to navigate reality. I used to tell my children that there were more dangerous people in the world than just the knife-wielding and gun-toting kinds. There is a more common, pedestrian kind of dangerous person who will waste your time, drain your energy, distract you, and pull you into their orbits before you're aware. This kind of person should be avoided. Unfortunately, the dangers of incoherent people can be even worse than this when they combine their powers. This group can destroy ecosystems, promote fear, greed, loathing, and xenophobia, and with the aid of technology, maybe even destroy societies. A few weeks ago it was revealed that an up-and-coming superpower nation had many more nuclear warheads than previously estimated, 300 more to be exact. David Bohm, who was an early contributing member of the Manhattan Project developing the nuclear bomb under Robert Oppenheimer, com-pared human evolution and cognitive coherence and was very concerned mankind's incoherence wouldn't know how to caretake such destructive potential.

Energy and Consciousness

What if we consider David Bohm's writing about energy, the universe, and matter and we extrapolate on them regarding consciousness? Bohm contended that what we consider to be the emptiness of space is really filled with energy, a plenum which connects everything and of which we are also part and connected. Matter—stars, planets, our physical bodies—all occupy this space, though to a lesser degree since the universe is mostly energy. Our mind is also dual configured in an energy/matter way but, like space, we are unaware of its dual equipping; we don't see it in this way.

Our conscious and unconscious mind and its borderless energy are hopelessly tethered to, bounded by, and preoccupied with the physical matter it embodies and searches for. This is comforting to our identity, since it makes us physical and tangible, real. But our unconscious mind and its energy specifically are also directly connected to and part of something larger, something more ethereal and not yet understood: a river of consciousness on which conscious thought only skims along the surface of. The closest our unconscious comes to physical matter as reality is probably during the creation of dreams.

Bohm says the vastness of space is mostly energy, of which matter (stars, planets, etc.) is only a small part. But the conscious material (matter) which become part of the mind, reflexive thought—with its identity construction, superficial material representations of itself and others, and material pursuits—is no more than a ripple on the surface of this vast river of consciousness. It makes up only a small part, yet this part is all pervasive, and takes on the whole of life. We would like to, and perhaps even try to, create an image of ourselves more attune and connected with the universe and everything within. But the *I* and the *me* of the self, our self-deceptive thoughts and incoherence, and the mental distractions of physical matter hold most of us prisoner from the light of such ideas.

Can we dive into this river and swim deep below the surface or are we destined to forever splash around the top? Does the energy of our mind have the power to travel distances, connect with other living things, or even cross the cosmos of space and time, but we are unaware or uninterested? Finally, if our energy came in contact with the right amounts of baryonic matter and stardust to create us again in another world, would a spark ignite and materially begin our physical selves anew?

Choosing Connection and Dealing with Messy

We live in an infinite, expansive universe, yet there is something in us that wants to separate, fragment, and divide everything. Whether the reason is the "I" and the "me" subject/object split of the self, our primal amygdala vs the limbic and prefrontal cortex brain, self-deceptive thoughts, or something else, we cannot be certain. However, I am certain you should get comfortable with words like *messy* and *unfinished* and then try your best to create *perfect* and *complete* within those borders and within the context of now, knowing you won't stay there long.

Also get comfortable with the idea that there is no ultimate answer. *Ultimates* and *perfects,* if they exist, are continual, con-textual, situational, embodied, and fleeting. They will have an expiration date. While this may make you feel unpopular or even wishy-washy in the face of others, it will ultimately garner you

174

respect from genuine leaders, as they know it's honest, authentic, and courageous. Learning to be comfortable with discomfort and ambiguity will help you get back into the driver's seat of "you" and relegate divisive and absolute thoughts to the back seat, turning them from definitive antagonists into a contributing member of perception.

PART 5:
START UNTHINKING

So we've been talking about and around the idea of *unthinking*—how to channel, clear a path and a place for, and use and honor the vast subconscious intuitive mind which mostly occupies the right hemisphere of our brain. We've talked about unthinking in business and in everyday life and how to create unthinking, and now we're going to talk about doing it, but we've really been talking about doing it throughout this book. As I suggested earlier, I could probably sell a million copies of this book if I wrote a checklist, self-help, step-by-step, "how to." But while life often is that easy, simple advice seldom works and doesn't stick. Why? Because you wouldn't be ready to take the advice, to take those steps, when first encountered; you wouldn't be transformed, prepared, and ready to receive the simple advice. You're still the same person you were yesterday. So while consuming such a book would taste great like a burger and fries, it would just be empty calories and you'd still be hungry afterward and not really fulfilled.

What's the alternative? When friends get together, they have a conversation. They don't make declarative statements or write out lists; they ask one another questions, listen, and tell stories. Let's continue our conversation between two friends and share interesting things and "what-if's" around the subject of unthinking, tapping into the intuitive mind, becoming more aware and self-aware, suspending judgment and impulse, and looking for, living, and sharing stories. Let's observe not just what's around us but also what's inside us (our thoughts) and then triangulate thoughts, awareness, and observation using the conscious and unconscious mind to navigate our best day, every day. Are you ready to unthink your way to a better life? Write to me in a year and tell me how your life has changed.

Scaling Exploration and Creativity in Times of Change

A recent study on intelligence conducted by NASA set out to determine what kinds of people scored highest in the category of creativity. The results were surprising. One demographic consistently scored in the 99th percentile, the "genius" level for creativity: they were kindergarteners. Perhaps more surprising, this was a longitudinal study conducted over time, and when the participants were retested at various points in their life, their scores decreased. By the time they were approaching adulthood, it seemed as if they were no longer geniuses in creativity. Somehow, they had lost their genius-level creativity.

American architect, futurist, and inventor Buckminster Fuller once said, "Everyone is born a genius, but the act of living de-geniuses us." It turns out he was right. This chapter discusses exploration in the creative sense and where it fits in our work, our life, and our world. How much exploration and explorative creativity (vs more exploitative pursuits) are good for us, and how much is frivolous or destructive? Who owns creativity, who should control it, and where should it be practiced, used, and applied? The answers to some of these questions may surprise you.

The terms *exploitation* and *exploration* refer to an organization's ability to do what it has traditionally learned to do well, "exploiting" the marketplace for profit and market share, and what it is able to learn and innovate anew, "exploring" the market for new growth and ultimately new exploitation. These terms describe a rare type of learning organization I've been researching for years known as an *ambidextrous organization*. For these dynamic organizations, scaling exploration and creativity is easy and natural; it's part of their life.

Full disclosure: The title of this section is a bit of a misnomer. First, it could easily be argued that creativity doesn't need scaling; it is infinite, unlimited, always present, and self-scaling. We humans, however, do just about everything in our power to hold it back, to descale it, even discourage and kill it. The title also refers to "times of change," suggesting we need to address creativity only at certain (changing) times. The reality is that we are always in a time of change; change is constant, continuous, and never ending. Therefore, we need to "always" be cognizant of the use of *creativity* and *exploration,* and, more importantly, we need to change our fundamental views of it and our relationships with it.

Exploration and Creativity as Limitless

Despite the fact that exploration and creativity are limitless, we still try to impose limits on them. Why? Forces (or, more correctly, people) decide in advance how far we will go in inquiry, discovery, and creativity, and then set about to regulate these endeavors according to some plan. In reality, creativity and exploration have no scale; they are infinite. The human mind and society will try to impose limits. So we can take exploration as far as we want to and build on creativity as elaborately as we like, but we might do it alone, or under oppression; it might be a struggle. It is *always* being moderated by limits. Advocates for control of creativity will argue this is a good thing, but I would counter that it's not. How's it been working for mankind so far?

Conversely, while we treat *exploration* and *creativity* (limitless things) as limited and in need of control, why do we treat *exploitation* and the repeat of the familiar as if it's endless and limitless? Through history, many giants of industry ultimately failed because they kept doing what they were doing after circumstances in the environment, surroundings, changed. The same happens to civilizations and to people. More desirable and superficially attractive, exploitation gets better press and marketing—in part because it is quantifiable and tangible; we know it and did it yesterday. Exploiting something is familiar ground; you're comfortable with it. But because exploitation is not limitless, eventually you'll exhaust it and use it up and must find something new. Yet we more often prefer this activity to our detriment, exercising it to exhaustion, over exploration, even when we intuitively know circumstances are changing and we need to stop and change.

The Limitless Universe and Our Limited Minds

I know this is up for debate, but at least for our intents and purposes the universe is limitless. Why, then, do we limit it? Part of the reason is that humans are not comfortable contemplating infinity. We crave borders and limits and need to know that we are bound, anchored, and secured to something. Even our very physiology and cognition is set up as a filtering receiver, taking some wavelengths of light into our eyes and not others, hearing some frequencies of sound but not others. We traditionally operate in narrow bandwidths.

These truths present some interesting contradictions. Though we humans have limits, in certain areas and conditions we like to act as if we don't, and in other areas where we are limitless, we self-impose limits. We like to think of ourselves as limitless in physical areas but limited in mental areas. These are the wrong perceived and imposed constraints. It's a backwards, fickle predicament. Additionally, most of us feel limitless when we're in a safe, comfortable setting and doing known, familiar things. Perhaps this is why we like to perpetuate exploitation and repeat familiar practices even if they're obsolete, inefficient, or destructive. And though we have limits, we will also heap more imposed limits upon ourselves, to the point of mentally or physically debilitating ourselves, shorting our power further. Humans are resilient, tough creatures, but also sensitive and fearful. We navigate with a filtered picture the best we can, and the surer we think we are about something, the more incorrect we might be.

Scales and Scaling

Scaling *exploration*, and *creativity*, should be as easy as scaling exploitation, but we treat it as a different operation altogether, and we have it reversed. In an exploitative (known) process, I produce 100 units at X location. Now I want to produce at Y, a second location. I produce 100 units daily at X; now I'll produce 200 units daily at X and Y, respectively. Easy when we're talking about the manufacturing of tangible goods. But do we do these kinds of calculations for exploration, imagination, or creativity? Do we apply this same kind of shrewdness and matter of fact logistics? Do we even consider that these same kinds of formulas could apply? No. It almost appears as if we've applied the same rules only in reverse. We consistently scale *down* creativity, scale down exploration and imagination, only to then make feeble attempts to resurrect and quickly promote or encourage them when we feel they're desperately needed, only to fail in our attempts. It's a proven neurological fact that the hippocampal volume in the brain decreases if we don't use imagination and creativity. But how do we scale these things responsibly, safely, joyfully, and without fear or guilt? By letting in and encouraging the intuitive unthinking mind to have a part in life.

Here's another disturbing conclusion regarding exploration and creativity. In businesses and organizations, they seem to be moderated by exploitation, when they should be endeavors unto themselves, with their own place and governance in the right hemisphere of the brain instead of being regulated by the left. Instead of subjugating the control of creativity and exploration to the mental (hemispheric) equivariant of a train conductor with a pocket watch, they need to be given their own seat at the grown-ups table alongside traditional exploitative practices. Why don't we do these things and why does society "de-genius" us from adolescence, discouraging and relegating creative exploration and imagination until it no longer has a legitimate voice?

Brigadier General Retired James (Scott) O'Meara, now a cross-functional problem solver and high-performance team builder, is currently working to introduce a technology "solution-based" business model into a long-term professional "service-based" model. During his military service, he led an exploratory project tasked with thinking about the military of the future. Scott said that today similar groups continue to look deeper in time, but senior leaders have long strived to have everyone think and write about the future. Achieving this contextual leveling up and down across large organizations may be an infinite goal and unreachable.

Scaling creativity and exploration, he suggests, tends to get pushed away by more exploitative core lines of business.

We have a difficult relationship with exploration and creativity, and furthermore we're most likely in denial of that fact. There is something in us that is both infinite and definite and it's conflicting, often leaving us not knowing which cards to play in our hand. We publicly deny exploration, creativity, and imagination, yet covet them, conceal them, disparage and are ashamed of them. It goes on and on. Each of us desires these things; we need them as much as we need the very air we breathe. Any way you look at it, it's a mess of judgment that needs to be reconciled before humanity can progress at a new faster pace.

Deciding on the right balance and how much exploration and creativity we should practice in our lives is both a personal choice and a decision for a larger society, but it scales up from you. A friend recently commented to me that reality is interpreted through individual lenses of experience. It's personal experience to the individual but it's cultural experience to an organization or society. Are you aware that you are simultaneously contributing to culture and yourself while you provide commentary about your organization or your life? Are you aware of the role you play on the stage of work and life in this regard? When you consider how much exploration, creativity, and imagination you want from life, ask how much others want and need, and want and need from you.

The Risk to Culture

Why are we talking about culture and risk in a discussion about creativity? Because culture sits squarely on the explorative and creative side of organizations, and is always at risk of damage, death, or transforming into something which could no longer be called culture. Just about everything in life can be reduced to a question of risk. Whether it's building a multimillion-dollar aircraft, having a discussion with your teenager about safe sex, or crossing a city street, it involves risk. In another life, one hat I wore was that of a "risk manager." My job, with the help of something called a "risk cube," was to determine the overall *likeliness* and *consequence* (along an X and Y axis) of doing, or not doing, various projects and activities. In my industry, the risk manager was the Rodney Dangerfield of jobs; it received little respect. But what if we had a "likeliness" and "consequence" risk cube for culture? What if we discussed the likelihood and consequences of not promoting creativity, not exploring, or not using imagination in an organization? A true ambidextrous (learning) organization would use this important tool as its risk manager once did in new ways to monitor, create, and protect fragile cultures and expose their hidden perils of spiritual death.

What's the Answer?

There is an optimal answer to scaling exploration, creativity, and imagination, but chances are if you're not already thinking about it, have had these thoughts previously, or are doing it, you're going to default back to a status quo tomorrow. We are creatures of habit, and changing things and ideas we didn't originally come up with causes us stress and upsets our apple carts. Regardless, I'm going to tell you to think about these things. Partly so I can say "I told you so" and partly because just maybe you'll listen and start taking these intuitive knocks on the door from the universe more seriously.

What is this thing I'm talking about specifically? In this case it's ambidexterity, ambidextrous thinking, and tapping into the intuitive, unthinking mind. It's finding an optimal balance between exploitation (doing what you already do well) and exploration (being explorative, creative, imaginative, and learning new things). Only you know what the right balance and rhythm is going to be for you, and I would argue that it's always a shifting balance. If the culmination of your life's story reads as one continual 90/10 split on one side or the other of the exploitation/exploration curve, you may have missed much of your precious life and gotten some important things wrong—even for those who spent 90% of their lifetime on the explorative creative side. Sadder still, if this *was* you, like the average person you probably carved the exploration, creativity, and imagination side out, and did it almost completely (relegating it to 10% of life or less), and traded it in for a pair of oars in the bottom of a ship. Since the brain is an organ that often behaves like a muscle, it will repeat patterns.

Who is the purveyor of "normal," at work and in life? Who gets to decide for you? The truest answer is you. Culturally, behaviorally, procedurally, activity wise, *what* should we "mostly" be doing with our limited time in this physical world? Exploiting it doing the familiar, exploring it for the new? Between being openly creative and focused on the new or being stationary in place, dwelling on the known, the answer is both, and it starts with putting exploration and creativity back into your life.

Here are four things you can start doing *right now* to get a better balance and rhythm back and be a beacon for others to do the same. A world radiates out from you if you allow it. Shine a light for others.

Validate the Universe

Validate the universe by validating what's good in it. After all, it works hard to validate you every day, and isn't it polite to repay a favor? Critical thinking makes rare appearances these days. When it does appear, it often goes unrecognized or unacknowledged.

Sometimes we are so busy trying to solve problems our own way that we talk over and past one another, or, heaven forbid, even get annoyed if someone ponders something out loud that invites us to think differently and break predetermined routine. Critical thinkers and their questions are too often dismissed or cast out of groups in favor of those who say things that appear to be smarter and more "get-things-done" action oriented. The reality is that these people are often regurgitating and advocating what everyone already knows; they're not asking or saying anything new. Tell someone if you like the different tack they're on or if it moves the needle or changes your view. It's important to stop briefly at those cognitive intersections and acknowledge the different. This is one way to validate the universe. For me, critical thinking most often makes its appearance as a question, and better questions lead to better answers. Punch someone's ticket once in a while with a validating question or comment (publicly if you can) and acknowledge their exploration, imagination, or creativity. The universe will respond in remarkable ways.

Be the Universe

It's been said that everyone is a universe unto themselves. If you think about it, we're made of all the same stuff: carbon, hydrogen, magnesium, lithium; we are literally made of extra-galactic matter. So, as a universe, make good things happen, lots of them. Here are a couple of things to try:

- Recognize someone publicly for something good they have done—and do it unexpectedly.

- Recognize someone privately for something good they have done and use frankness, candor, and personal sharing and do it unexpectedly.

- Be someone's first follower. An important part of distinction is the first person who considered *you* distinctive, and the *first follower* is perhaps the most distinctive person of all to them. It takes a great deal of courage to be first at something. Being the first one to hike down a trail takes guts; recognizing someone for distinction before anyone else or when others don't feels just as risky. Most will ignore the idea of being first to recognize another because they (the person) don't come from a previously vetted, "safe" place, because they feel uncomfortable, or because they're trapped in a zero-sum game that won't allow them to validate or celebrate another publicly lest they be diminished or over-shadowed themselves. Ask yourself what you would lose by tooting the horn for someone else's talent, accomplishment, or idea. Do you have the courage to be a first follower, celebrating another's awesomeness?

- Give someone your absolute undivided attention, listen, and ask questions. Unexpectedly tell them they're on the right path, did a great job, and tell them the reasons why.

Get to a Creative Space

Get to a creative space and help others get there, even if you have to drag them kicking and screaming. Filmmaker Alfred Hitchcock's bulldog Geoffrey often helped his master and his writing team get into a creative space where story ideas would begin to flow, much to the chagrin of his young staff who were most interested in coming up with writing ideas quickly. When Hitchcock's team sat down to discuss ideas, Hitchcock often began with a completely irrelevant story of Geoffrey's morning walk through the garden and the sights, sounds, and smells he encountered there—even to the detail of which flowers he preferred to sniff and which he preferred to relieve himself on. These seemingly inane (TMI) stories had an important point and purpose: they helped the team shift their thinking and get to a creative space. Those in the know recognize that creativity takes a transitory preparation of 20 to 30 minutes. It requires priming and the right environment. Prepare a place for others to imagine, create, and explore.

Fight Cynicism

I've talked about this in articles before, and it's worth repeated mention because cynicism seriously cobbles and shuts down exploration, creativity, and imagination. Cynicism, said former U.S. Secretary of Defense James Mattis, "sows fear, distrust, and isolationism." Mattis wrote an opinion piece on cynicism easily found if searched for which is worth the read. He commented: "Our politics are paralyzing the country [in this instance the USA]. We practice suspicion or contempt where trust is needed, imposing a sentence of anger and loneliness on others, and ourselves. We scorch our opponents with language that precludes compromise and brush aside the possibility that a person with whom we disagree might be right. We talk about what divides us and seldom acknowledge what unites."

What is dangerous, he said, is not that people have serious differences; instead, it's the tone—the snarl, the scorn, and the lacerating despair. Mattis contended that cynicism is cowardice, and it is corrosive when it saturates a society. Everyone benefits from understanding other points of view, but cynicism fractures organizations because people hunker down, build defenses, stop questioning and being open minded, and stop exploring and being creative. About politics, Mattis said that too often we define our great national challenges—climate change, immigration, health care, guns—in a way that guarantees division into warring camps. Instead he said, we should be asking one another: What can "better" look like?

Mattis attested that the short-term thinking that cynicism promotes tends toward a selfish *"better get mine while I can"* attitude, killing long-term thinking, which plays to higher ideals and requires creativity, exploration, and strategic thinking. Finally, and perhaps most disturbingly, Mattis said cynicism fosters a distrust of reality, and if you can drive a wedge in the definition of reality, you can suggest a new one. Cynics create a bully pulpit to insert their own point of view, whatever that is. Mattis finished by saying, "Virulent, take-no-prisoners attacks on the media, the judiciary, labor unions, universities, teachers, scientists, civil servants—pick your target—don't help anyone. When you tear down institutions, you tear down the scaffolding on which society is built." While Mattis said "institutions," he meant organizations and people, and, as he said, "pick your target."

The threat of cynicism isn't simply a threat to reality but is also a threat to the very energy of the universe. Energy we would otherwise spend exploring is instead diverted to shoring up. Energy spent being creative is spent narrowing focus, hoarding, taking assessment and inventory, and refining what we already did rather than on new connections and discoveries we would make tomorrow. Our thinking moves from one of a mix of strategic (long term) and tactical (short term) to all short term (tactical). When this happens, we lose sight of tomorrow, and our future becomes relegated to yesterday. Fight cynicism.

Keep Moving Toward Hard

John Wayne said: "Life is hard. It's even harder when you're stupid." He was right. Things are going to be tough for you until you get smarter and conquer the hard. What's the definition of hard (and stupid) for me? It's not having a clear understanding of yourself in a living embodied contextual world. Everything else is just ignorance borne of a specific lack of knowledge and is forgivable.

Laurie Santos, a Yale professor who teaches the university's most popular course in history, on the science of happiness, offered tips for knowing yourself. Santos said knowing your core character strengths can help you to get, and stay, in the zone in work and life and experience, what researchers call "flow." You can take a University of Pennsylvania survey online to discover what your strengths are. Besides curing you of your stupidity, what else could this do for you? Santos said knowing what you're most passionate about may very well allow you the ability to find what's often referred to as "your calling," that activity that puts you in a perpetual state of flow.

Pulling It All Together

There's a famous observation attributed to Einstein: "If I had an hour to solve a problem, I'd spend 55 minutes thinking about the problem and 5 minutes thinking about solutions." At this time in human history, we do the exact opposite: we spend 55 minutes discussing the implementation of yesterday's solutions with 5 minutes allocated to what the true nature of the problem might be. This common scenario is the kind of exercise where exploration, creativity, and imagination would pay big dividends. And if you do it Einstein's way, the intuitive unthinking mind will be at your side accompanying you in the process.

Whether it's fighting cynicism, encouraging exploration, legitimizing creativity, using imagination, or embracing change, the answer to successfully scaling these things in times of change, or anytime, is *you*. And when you learn to vanquish the foes and cultivate and harvest the gifts, it will be you running on all cylinders, mentally, physically, and spiritually. The world needs you here at this moment in time. It needs you awake, lucid, intelligent, and intelligible. And it needs you doing the right kinds of things.

Surviving Fear and Moving Forward

A few chapters ago we discussed "The New Disrupter," addressed the COVID-19 pandemic and how this virus has changed our lives in unexpected and revolutionary ways. I even labeled it as a new kind of organizational ambidexterity—conscripted, one with a *mandatory enrollment* that truly presented both peril and new opportunities to reengineer the 21st century for you and everyone.

I've written about ambidexterity a lot and even wrote a book about it in 2019. The balancing of exploitation and exploration in business, and in life, is an important topic for all of humanity. This fourth kind of organizational ambidexterity I introduced beyond *temporal, spatial,* and *contextual* is distinctively different because, at least for a time, it has had us in its grip, forcing us to change our behavior and thinking.

An interesting article I read not too long ago reminded me of a sentiment the late organizational researcher James March once shared: "If you want to win, you will employ exploration. If you want to avoid losing, you will employ exploitation." Transfer that to the conscripted (change or die) ambidexterity introduced by the 2020 pandemic and that saying might sound like this: "If you want to survive and win, employ exploration." Traditionally, we usually employ exploitation because it's familiar and therefore less risky and guarantees faster results, but it doesn't guarantee a "tomorrow." Exploration, by comparison, involves risk and is not assured. The interesting thing about the pandemic is that it caused us to employ both strategies in earnest and in equal amounts—maybe to a perfect 50/50 balance or even higher in its percentage of exploration.

Will we sustain these healthier ratios? The important takeaway here is that in the process of being forced into changes, we will discover and learn new things that may and will be better for us, better for humanity, and better for the entire planet. Whether we incorporate these changes as permanent or go back to a variation of the old ways is up to us. But make no mistake: the course of humanity and reality has shifted and changed forever. You are now in a new world, and you have also changed. With these changes and unknowns comes fear, some of it healthy perhaps, but most of it unnecessary, contrived, and unfortunate. Let's look at the current new environment and learn to do the things we've previously done but do them better, and do the things we've only dreamed of doing for the very first time.

What's Going On?

What's going on within us in regard to fear is kind of like what happens to retired astronauts no longer flying in space or prisoners of war released from captivity. We experience confusion, depression, loss of identity, hesitation, and fear, resultant from a dramatic shift of habit, even when shifting to better habits or circumstances. It's like we are standing at the edge of a cliff, a precipice, of radical change, teetering on an abyss, and it's a terrifying feeling for everyone, even ex-astronauts. When this happens, in addition to feeling paralysis, we also conversely want to jump into action, and when we do, we frequently get into trouble. We think the "pre-jump" view we have of our situation is a complete and correct picture, but usually it's not. We get ourselves into error chains that get worse until they're broken. Ask any of my former coworkers in aviation about error chains and they will tell you hair-raising stories. When we act prematurely, we double down on our decisions and are quick to build assumptions and judgments from our actions, which can last years or have lasting effects.

In addition to our personal human nature there is also something transitional and transformational going on in the world. At times it can feel as if the entire world is on fire, but that's just one (negative) perspective. What's really happening is change. When the climate of our external environment gets anxious, it doesn't help our personal outlook; it just adds misleading confirmation bias. Heaven help me, but to this point I sometimes wonder if most of the media is a personification of negativity, or at the least being manipulated by cynicism. Of late, it appears like the mainstream media is continually and desperately trying to get, or regain, control of our attention by showing us the worst humanity has to offer in frightening parables along with endless examples of how the earth is increasingly flicking us off its back like a dog scratching at bothersome fleas. Make no mistake, there is a war going on, and it's an internal and external war—for our attention, and control of our fight-or-flight amygdala, using anything that triggers our fears. Bottom line, the world is not unraveling; it's simply a battle for attention, control, and perspective.

Nothing Personal; It's Just a Control Thing

So if these cataclysms aren't the beginning of Armageddon, then what are they? Control maneuvers. As humans, we fret over this a lot. Whether it's losing it, gaining it, having it, giving it, having it imposed upon us, or sharing it, it takes up a lot of our precious time, and companies are no different. They spend much of their time and resources trying to figure out how to best administer control and how much to dispense to get the maximum productivity and performance from a workforce. A wise, slightly wry coworker once told me, "Companies hire you for one of two reasons. You either make them money or you save them money." And to do these things, they feel the need to keep you under control.

I like to show a chart to students when I teach. It sparks great conversation and offers an interesting pragmatic perspective. It was first introduced to me by one of my George Washington University professors, Dave Schwandt. This chart by Barley and Kunda shows what are called *rational* and *normative* forms of workplace control through history. Simply put, it shows cyclical eras or movements in history from *objective and scientific* (rational and logical), to *humanistic and social* (normative, intuitive, and emergent) regarding how best to control workers. Coming out of agrarian, theologian, and artisan societies on the far left of the chart, humans entered the industrial revolution and there was immediately a need to embrace mechanized technology and meld man with machine. *Industrial betterment* in the humanistic normative movement was code for "you can't physically beat and abuse people in factories to make them productive, and they need health benefits and safe working places." Labor unions began to emerge during this era. Next was the *scientific management* movement sparked by Frederick Taylor and his stopwatch calculating *maximum efficiency*, attempting to get perfect mechanized efficiency from a workforce. Next, interestingly, the *human relations* movement of the 1920s started our modern-day HR departments, and many are still dual-hatted, developing, mentoring, and training workers while also administering control, benefits packages, hiring, and counseling employees. Where are we now in regard to this chart? It seems like we are (or were) in a rational, more pragmatic movement, and more disconnected from human feelings and social mores, and more connected to rational, logical thinking—but that may be quickly changing.

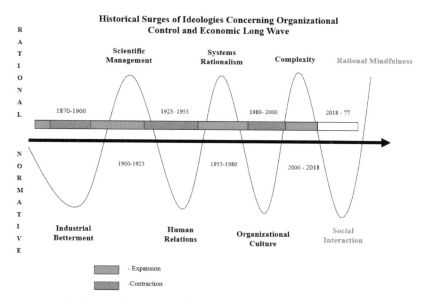

Barley, S.R. and Kunda, G. (1992) "Design and devotion: Surges of rational and normative ideologies of control in managerial discourse. ASQ 37(3) Modified by Professor David Schwandt for GW University (2010), updated/modified by E. Zabiegalski for Webster University HR Training and Development, and Management course (2018)

Then came the COVID-19 pandemic and the environmental disruption it created. Telework, something that for decades only got lip service, was suddenly, reluctantly allowed. Telework was largely unregulatable, so workers had to be trusted, a risky endeavor, and companies found they were more productive in surprising ways.

New conversations started from old theories like Douglas McGregor's 1950s Theory X and Y. In managers' eyes, employees were either dirtbags (Theory X) and needed to be monitored 24/7 or they would sluff off work and steal the store. Or they were guided by an internal compass toward excellence (Theory Y), doing their best, and left to their own devices they would do the right thing. Which side of this debate are you on and why do you feel that way?

Suddenly, there were critical shortages in traditionally low-paying jobs and many no longer wanted to be controlled in traditional ways or go back to work in conventional ones. There was also a quiet movement to push leadership and management down to the lowest levels of organizations, creating more self-led and self-managed workers who are empowered to get the job done, with leaders and managers serving to run interference and remove obstacles in the way of these empowered employee-leaders' success.

A few years ago, I left my traditional service company to be part of an ESOP (employee stock ownership plan) company. These companies give workers ownership interest in their organizations and by virtue of that take a novel and different approach to controlling and balancing organizations. The theory goes like this. As employee-owners, there is less of a need to enact rational or normative controls in the company, or perhaps they're more normative. Workers (employees) are more closely aligned with their own self-interest and empowerment and don't need as much external incentivization to perform. They are inherently more self-managed, self-led, self-fulfilled, self-aware, and self-controlled.

Built for Continual Change

With so much rapid change going on in the world, there is some solace. Though we don't seem to like it very much, we can take comfort in the knowledge that we also operate well in continual change and transition. It's literally in the cells of every organ of our bodies.

A recent article on neuroscience said our brains need to be flexible to learn new things but also need to consistently represent the known world around us. Until now, scientists have largely found that specific neurons within the brain fire off when a specific smell is smelled or a specific sight is seen, and they're always the same neurons. In other words, these neurons are dedicated to their particular stimulus and experiences. But it's turning out this isn't necessarily true. With the discovery of something called *"representational drift,"* it has been discovered that while some neurons refire after time passes and a familiar sensation is sensed, others that previously did, don't anymore. They move on and will now respond to other sensations.

How can animals possibly make any lasting sense of the world if their neural responses to that world are always in flux? How does the brain know what the nose is smelling or what the eyes are seeing if the neural responses to smells and sights are continuously changing? It might be that while some neurons change, a few remain the same, hang back, or collectively they retain some aspect of memory even though they have moved on to new things. Think of a tour group that moves to the next exhibit in a museum while a few stay behind and linger. The entire group has a consensus of what they just saw while moving on to the next experience. Is this a bug in our nervous system, an evolutionary flaw? This representational neural drift might be beneficial and help us. Drift could be a manifestation of learning. By constantly changing how information is stored and shuffled around, the nervous system may be better able to accommodate new learning and material. There is something going on here that we don't yet understand, and we have no existing theories for comparison.

Along with classical physics, we developed the laws of quantum mechanics to tell us why sometimes things did not behave as they should when scaled down. Currently there are no "work-around" theories like quantum physics and mechanics in neuroscience. With all that we've learned, neuroscience still has many vague and cloudy areas as a field of research. Neurons are more understood than the operation of larger neural networks. According to some theorists, stable neural representations have never been a theory, but have been more of a tacit assumption and probably a desire, because it makes more intuitive sense and is more comforting. As humans, we want and even need to see things as fixed, stable, and predictable, but the world tells us more often than not that everything is in continual flux. The field of neuro-science is still conceptually immature, and researchers are hungry for theories. Scientists are now interested in finding places in the brain where representational drift *doesn't* happen. Are there such places?

Responses

So the world and universe are evolving and changing rapidly, and we are part of this tumultuous transformation. We could even be entering a dawn of an incredible new age for humankind and not be aware of it. Like I said earlier, do you think a fish knows it's swimming in water? What can we do to enjoy this whitewater and successfully get down river to the ocean? Try adopting these things.

Take Back Control

Retired NASA astronauts have a program designed for them to fight depression and the stress it causes. Why are they depressed? These celestial athletes go from 60 to 0 when they leave the space program and enter civilian life. This represents a rapid deceleration in activity, identity, and life. There are programs like this for veterans too like The Honor Foundation, of which I am a mentor and coach.

The pandemic did the same thing to us, and on a global scale. Instead of happening to a few dozen astronauts or vets, an existential existence-jarring shift happened to 7.8 billion humans around the world. This mean that there are a lot of dazed and confused people walking around, so you're not alone if you feel like a wreck. What can you do to take back control (or perhaps gain it for the first time), moving forward and living your best life? One important thing is to reacquaint yourself with yourself and then double down on that original, pure version of you.

Regarding alcohol, I'd always been a weekend social drinker, with a couple of beers on a Friday after work and Saturday while standing at the BBQ grill. When the COVID-19 pandemic hit, I suddenly found myself drinking every day. Was this a manifested exploitative behavior on my part? Was it becoming too frequent of a habit? I began to wonder if I was developing a problem. When I began to think about it and reflected that I had been drinking alcohol for decades, it concerned me anew. "What kind of person was I when I was 12, when I didn't drink alcohol?" I wondered. If I hadn't developed an alcoholism problem, maybe I had developed a coping mechanism for avoiding challenges, incivilities, and cruelties of life. I decided I wanted to go back to that original self and meet that person again, so I stopped drinking alcohol for 18 months.

That change gave me back much of my peace of mind and a different, new form of control of my days and weeks. The things that matter most in life are real connections, awareness, unobstructed connection with feelings (be they good or bad), being helpful and present, and navigating the good, bad, and indifferent of the day. One controlling way that personal experiment changed me was to change the sinusoidal wave (sine wave) of my behavior from week to week from one of wide swings daily or weekly to one that was longer and shallower. Coincidentally, three powerful books discussing personal control that were written at the dawn of the self-help age (and around the same time as the human resources movement began in business that we discussed) are *As a Man Thinketh*, by James Allen, *How to Win Friends and Influence People*, by Dale Carnegie, and *Think and Grow Rich*, by Napoleon Hill. These books all lay down principles, advice, and a course of action that are often timeless, genuine, and human.

Manage Your Personal Stock

You must authentically *"be"* you before you can *"do"* you. This can be difficult if you've never been sure who "you" are or have become as an adult, if you have lost sight of who that person is. It's entirely possible that the years have challenged your perception of you, and you've become lost. Checking on and managing your personal stock is a good way to get back on track and end the agonizing feeling of being insignificant, afraid, and helpless. Are you in good standing among others? Is your personal stock valuable and on the rise? If you know who you are, that answer is always yes.

One way to find out and get back on track is to understand something important about you. In a great TED Talk, Kathleen Taylor, a hospice counselor, challenges us to rethink the traditional *bucket list*. She has talked with many individuals at the end of their lives about their regrets and successes and has come up with some surprising commonalities and discoveries. She said you are the only one in the universe, which is constellated specifically in the way you are; you truly are one of a kind. Though you are one of a kind, your unique configuration also fits like a puzzle piece with all the other constellations in the universe, other people. It's astounding we should ever feel alone or lost once we know this, she contends. Though we are unique individuals, we are also part of a larger set. We are all part of one symphony, but you are the only one playing your particular note.

She offers this advice to those not sure of their value. Instead of asking what I should be doing with my life, we should be asking, "who am I being with my life?" The idea here is that the "being" comes first and is later met at the intersection of "doing." You bring the "being" with you; that's inherently yours and it's portable. You have always had it and always will. No one gave it to you, and no one can take it from you. The truly wonderful thing about this is that when you meet *doing* at that crossroad, you will *"do"* with your *"being."* And that will be truly unique. Naturally, you never have to be afraid of losing it, of it being devalued or having it taken from you. You call the plays here, you're in control, you own all the stock. Isn't that amazing? The complete work, the music of this giant cosmic symphony, wouldn't happen without your unique note.

Kick Your Own Bucket

Kick your own bucket—your "bucket list" bucket, that is. The idea of the bucket list is something we're all familiar with. Dennis Pitocco, a friend who runs a LinkedIn publishing site called *Bizcatalyst 360*, of which I am proud to be a contributing writer, recently asked his readership a question: What's in your bucket? In asking people this traditional question, Dennis put a contemporary spin on it: What's your design, your unique collection? It doesn't have to be a list. What was my answer? Going forward, I said, I would like to trade possessions for experiences. I would like to use my credentials for human connection, and I would like to begin living my life in reverse, going back to someone I was originally when I began this journey.

"Don't wear fear or nobody will know you're there." —Cat Stevens, "Don't Be Shy," 1971

Be Brave

Stopping fear is easy. It's a simple decision, an agreement with yourself, and you've taken a big step to getting back into the driver's seat of your life by reading this. Now you just have to go out and do it. Everyone and everything has an agenda and an intent, and that's not necessarily bad; sometimes it's quite enjoyable and helpful. But you need to train your brain to look for and discern it, and to know what it is. Whether the agenda is universal and natural or manmade, you need to understand and unpack it, and then you can make some quick decisions about it and continue about your day. I'm not talking about cynicism here or being Machiavellian, just healthy practicality. The better you understand your organization, yourself, others, society, and your world, the better you can navigate around in it and be a force for good in it, wherever you go and in whatever you do.

How can this advice help? Regarding the work you do, before you commit to an organization, research the company's stated values, mission, and culture, and then bump that up against what's really happening in their hallways. Are the two congruent? Now compare that to your values, mission, and culture. Do they jibe? Bottom line, it's important for you to understand your company's worldview, even if the company itself doesn't understand it or think they have one. Such an understanding can save you a lot of wasted time and grief investing in a company you don't believe in, and it will enrich your experience, making you a better and more successful employee. Friend and occasional collaborator Eric Gafford, chairman of Gulfstream Aerospace's Community of

Experts, said that if you want to know what a company is like, "ask current employees what their opinions are and spend some time checking under the hood, and don't underestimate when you find that 'good fit.'"

Finally, realize control "is just a control thing," and it's not personal, frightening, or mean; it's simply human nature. Whether it's the media and politicians trying to terrify you into submission or specific action, a world in flux, or nervous organizations trying to ensure you perform duties according to contract, understand that ultimately you are in control and call the shots. You were designed for learning, change, and growth. Be honest, be brave, be helpful, and have fun with life!

Summing Up: What You Can Do

What can you do to connect with David Bohm's undivided wholeness more frequently, behave less incoherently, pick a worldview that can serve as a lifelong compass, and tap into the infinite wisdom of an intuitive unthinking subconscious mind, making it your wingman no matter where you go and what you do? Plenty! This last chapter summarizes some of the themes presented throughout this book and suggests a few last actionable steps which will soon work their way into your muscle memory, will be reflexively practiced by you, and surprisingly, will be noticed and commented on by others.

Think from the River's Source

Why do we kick people off our metaphoric bus? It's complicated, but much of it has to do with the way each of us chooses to see reality. These perceptions are complex and can be *very* different from one person to another. Deepak Chopra in his book *Metahuman* said, "Our day-to-day reality is inauthentic and compromised by the limiting mental and social frameworks that we impose upon it." We impose a lot. There is a meta reality (a reality beyond the layered identity we create) that exists outside of the interpretations that humans add, and it's extremely difficult to get to. Our mind-made reality isn't just made up of all the data that gets filtered through our senses; it's also made up of all the ideas and impressions that we filter through a complex matrix of beliefs. Chopra went on to say, "We persistently translate immaterial concepts into material forms; tangible, physical concrete things." Anything that manifests in the material world—a shirt button, a painting, an automobile—first started in the mind of an individual. We then celebrate, attend to, and hold on high those, and our, creations (what we have manifested). That's why office spread-sheets become so important, and it's why the highest-paying jobs in the world all deal with creations, and the creators and purveyors of concrete tangible things.

The uncomfortable (and wonderful) truth regarding reality and our physical and spiritual expression is that while part of us may seem stationary and fixed, we are also constantly changing, transient beings. But we assign fixed characteristics to one another and ourselves rather than considering new iterations and possibilities and our capability for change, learning, and growth. While we think defining and locking down our identities helps us cope, it also limits our potential, and we get caught in a tangled network of beliefs, social frameworks, mental conditioning, experiences, and opinions. Like the things we physically manifest, our sense of self also becomes *reified* (converted into a concrete thing), even to the extent of identifying with our creations. When we do this, we deny ourselves our true infinite potential and delimit and descope ourselves and others. Perhaps there is no place where this is done more often than in the workplace and in our societies.

Earlier, I discussed a meta reality beyond the everyday world, a reality above the one we live in every day. Layers collected over decades of experiences, opinions, circumstances, and actions define, bound, and border who we become. The true meta reality of "us" is like an original clear spring we originate from rather than the muddy, overgrown delta we ultimately are after years of living. If we could strip away the vegetation, wash away the dirt, filter out and clean away the sediment, toxins, and debris, and remove the distractions, we would see more clearly what we are at our core from that original stream.

Unthink

Physicist David Bohm once said the brain is filled with "electrochemical smog." He was right. There is a generative order to the universe, in biology and life, but we (humans) inherently introduce misinformation into this order through our thoughts and in our minds. We multiply this misinformation, and this information, good or bad, helps to organize our order, the way in which we are made up. The first thing we can do to clear this smoke is to take back control of our thoughts and our mind.

What would you do if I told you one day in casual conversation to "unthink"? You'd probably look at me funny and then wouldn't know what to do with such strange advice. It might even cause you to incur more thinking as you would occupy your mind with trying to figure what I meant and how exactly to do it (unthink). But this is precisely what I'm prescribing, and I'm asking you to start doing it from this moment on. What do I mean when I say *unthink*? While you may think I have not told you or taught you exactly to your satisfaction how to do this thing called unthinking, I would reply that this is by intent and design. The solutions to unthinking have at once both commonalities to us all and ones that will be specifically unique to you. So for that reason, I have talked about those commonalities, hinted as to a path, and perhaps talked more about unthinking as an experience and a way of being than as a thing that is done. The answers to clearing a path for, channeling, and benefiting from an unthinking mind can be found hidden throughout this book. Some of them are in plain sight, some concealed and hidden, some spoken of directly, some alluded to, and some yet to be discovered when you've put this book down and all but forgotten about it.

As you read through these final pieces of advice, remember that we are most *right* when we are in motion, cognitive and physical motion. When we are in a state of learning, we know vastly more than when we park on a thought, an act, or a data point.

Realize You Are Not Your Brain

You are not your brain; you are the user of your brain—and hopefully you're its master. Someone once said we are not physical beings who occasionally have spiritual experiences. Instead, we are spiritual beings continually having a physical experience. These physical meat-suits we walk around in and this physically material world we perceive all around us are all-pervasive. They are in our face all the time, 24/7, giving us little respite for reflection, and the physical mechanical compartments and neurons in our brain (those charged with navigating and manipulating the material and physical) encourage and perpetuate this behavior, a behavior fixed and focused on the material and the physical. After all, it's the experience we're having. Physically speaking, two aspects make up our brain: a material side that is chemical with neurons, grey matter, mass, etc., and a consciousness side beyond the physical which is electrochemical, made of energy, and perhaps even immortal, living beyond us and after us. Regarding thought, there are also two sides of the brain which offer us two very different views of the world. One, predominantly residing in the left hemisphere, is a rational, conscious side, which prefers a mechanistic view of the world. Abstract, decontextualized, disembodied, and static, its thinking is like a water bug skimming on the surface of consciousness. It concerns itself more with the apprehension and navigation of a physical world than anything else. The other, predominantly comprising the right hemisphere, is more tied to intuition and gut feeling. Seeing the world in a living embodied contextualized moving landscape, this side is more "big picture" and has a disposition for the living more than the inanimate or the mechanical. Interestingly, psychologist Dr. Iain McGilchrist points out that damage sustained to either side of these hemispheres would still allow an individual to live and function using only the other, though their view of reality and the world may be radically different from ours. Additionally, if the damage happened to be on the right side of the brain, leaving the patient to have to rely on only the left hemisphere to live, there would be a dramatically greater chance of their suffering from schizophrenia. As Dr. McGilchrist explains it, these people wouldn't be irrational; having lost all of their rationality, rationality would be the only thing they had left.

Park on Values

Relevantly speaking, when it comes to what we stand on and stand for, a lot of people park on knowledge, but frankly that's an illogical and incoherent stance, and it's a little bit ridiculous. Park on what you value that brings you current knowledge in the first place: learning. Knowledge is a fleeting thing; it's constantly changing and being updated, validated, and invalidated. True knowing represents continuous learning. If you're wielding knowledge around like a sword or stacking it like sandbags around your desk, then you don't really care about truth, or what's right—only about you and winning. To determine what you truly value, ask yourself the same question my friend, Dr. Rob Bogosian, asks each of his MBA students: "What do you value more, knowing or learning?" That may be a trick question. Personally, I value learning, discovering, and sharing what I've learned with others more than facts and data. If you learn something you know it, but there's a different feeling in most workplaces. Facts and figures are king. They're useful and have power, but they should be the surprise and reward of exploration and discovery, the icing on the cake. This is true for individuals but not organizations.

When Rob asks his students this question, he asks it twice— first asking them what they value more, and then asking them what they think their organization values more. He invariably gets polarized answers. This difference represents a contradiction that has plagued organizations for over a century and will likely continue. Organizations aren't very collectively smart when it comes to learning, and they will likely never admit their Achilles heel. Though they may not figure out what *learning organization* really means or the benefits it can bring, it doesn't mean you also have to languish in this twilight. You can personally reconcile this easily by stopping and focusing on the part of knowledge that feels important (the learning) and not worrying about the rest. Let the accountants and managers figure that out, what you and your team discovered. Data points, facts, and figures are great, but they're just that—today's numbers, facts, and figures, and frankly lifeless abstract things with a short expiration without scrutiny, updating conversation, and application.

If you want to be right and always knowing, be always learning. That means, among other things, to always be moving. Focus on building a learning organization by focusing on people and their learning as opposed to data, numbers, and spreadsheets.

Strive for Perception

Strive for perception, not just thought (that voice in your head). Remember our talk about proprioception? That's what I'm talking about here. It's intuition, gut feeling, and the voice in your head. The greatest perception is achieved when awareness and observation consult with thought; that's proprioception and unthinking.

Make More Distinctions and Less Divisions

What's the difference between a division and a distinction? For one thing, divisions dig channels, put up walls, and separate that which we feel needs to be permanently separated. Distinctions, on the other hand, alert us to differences and unique qualities. While they may be like divisions in that they show borders, they're not boundaries. They're more permeable than permanent and are not designed to divide. The organized left hemisphere brain loves divisions, to the point that if our peas touch our carrots on our dinner plates, it could send us into a tizzy. In a world and universe which is one giant relational and connected ecosystem, our minds are continually busy making sure everything is kept apart.

Get Over Yourself and Then Start a Reformers Club

There's nothing like a group of reformed smokers to help you quit smoking. We've talked a lot about thought, identity, perception, and coherence and have concluded that even on our best days, we can get sorely played by our brain and its self-deceiving thoughts. No more. It's a confusing, complicated, mixed-up world we live in. Don't add to this mess by contributing another confusing, complicated, mixed-up, and scared person to it. I'm talking about you.

A big part of striving to live our best lives is knowing, showing, and being ourselves, and passing that authenticity on for others to model. The good news about admitting and living such a mess is that you will never get bored. When everything you do and every encounter is a puzzling challenge with a best solution to find, your life has purpose: to get better. It's important for you to see life, and struggle, and yourself in this way, and just get over yourself and your ego and the idea that you can't show mistakes or weakness or learning. There's a rare club for gritty, transparent, self-deprecating group learners who are quick to admit they screwed up or don't know how, and then learn how, and succeed. They're called leaders.

Find Your Guide

In much of this book, the brilliant physicist David Bohm shared his advice, with me pitching in. Expect this to also happen throughout your life: temporary and specific guides will come and go as you need them. But finding a permanent lifelong guide is really a trick of the mind exercise I use periodically to step back and more objectively take in the whole picture of my thoughts, behavior, and actions.

Here's how it works. Where is the center of you? Your consciousness? Where do you feel your "being" is, resides? Some say it's in the center of the chest, the solar plexus, while others say it's in the head. Still others will say they are able to move it through using focus, meditation, or concentration. All of these are true. One of the things consciousness allows us is the ability to step outside ourselves using our self-awareness. Consciousness is an *awareness of our own awareness*. With this knowledge and practice of self-awareness, I have learned to step back, away from myself, creating a spiritual guide to walk with me when I need it, through difficult decisions and times of precarious or perilous navigation. Try it and see what happens.

Keep Your Connection Clear and Open

You're always connected to wholeness, to what David Bohm calls the implicate order, but your conscious mind and subconscious mind are usually blocked from each other and blocking a continuous view. That's normal. For whatever reason, we humans are compelled to move away from wholeness and the implicate order, create divisions, and create abstractions (made up things) to clutter and fill the path. We like to push away from one another and the universal wholeness of life and venture out independently like babies taking their first steps. We fight and look for recognition and validation of our declared independence, even as we know it's all self-deception. No one is successful on their own; we all stand on the shoulders of giants. If we were to be raised away from humanity, we would not be human, but we support the delusion of independence and love the myth of the lone hero, leader, or achiever. Why we do this is unclear. Perhaps in an expanding universe where everything is moving away from everything else, we are compelled to do it as well. Are we wired this way in a universe doing the same? You can hedge yourself against this and other self-deceptions by keeping your link to wholeness unobstructed. Keep in mind you'll likely fail at times; you won't keep a perfect connection to wholeness all the time. That's okay. You're human, and maybe that's natural and meant to be. Just do your best and bring your "A "game to each day.

Help Others and Question Everything

If I could give you one piece of advice, it is to be helpful to others, selflessly helpful. A second piece of advice is to get in the habit of questioning everything around you—your desires, your decisions, your passion, the status quo, what you see, everything. Question it silently (inwardly) or vocally (outwardly) but do it often.

Make Your Dog Your Amygdala

Joking with my adult daughter one day, she asked if I intended to take her Chow dog, Wamu, with me on a trip to the hardware store. I told her that her anxiety-ridden, hyper alert, and slightly neurotic but sweet dog never let me out of his sight for an instant and might actually fall apart if I disappeared, so of course I was planning on taking him. He's my best buddy anyway, I added. "As a matter of fact," I said, "*I think* that *he thinks* he's my protector, so I'm going to pretend he's my amygdala for a day and see what happens." Our primal part of our brain, the amygdala, is chiefly concerned with our protection (fight or flight) and eliminating threats to us. As a result, it is always bugging us, alerting us, while we're trying to get other things done. If my daughter's dog picks up that job, and I no longer have to worry about it, maybe I'll be more relaxed and less stressed.

Here's the funniest part of this story. The minute I proposed this strategy to my daughter, I instantly felt as if a weight was lifted from my shoulders. I felt freer, lighter, more clear-headed, and instantly more relaxed. I looked over to Wamu, who was lying at my side looking up with loving eyes. After delegating my survival to my Chow, life became more relaxed. Try this trick and put someone or something else besides you in charge of your security for a day and see how it feels.

Keep It Real

Keep it as real as you can keep it. When discussing his life journey from a questioning adolescent to physicist and explorer of human consciousness, David Bohm spoke extensively about the limitations of the human mind. He spoke about how important it is for us to acknowledge these limitations, to know something of them, and to question the machinations and intrigue of a tirelessly working brain. The chief antagonist of our limitations is *desire*, Bohm says, which leads to self-deceptive thoughts. Bohm attests that most of man's thoughts are self-deceptive, tailored to rationalize why we do things and want things. In life, we will have desires, and these will most likely create our biggest problems. Bohm said we create self-deceptions to justify the objects we crave (the objects of our desire), and this thoughtless pursuit, this self-deception, leads to incoherence, unintended consequences, and irrationality.

Bohm said what we are really searching for in the pursuit of desires is a state of perfection, harmony, and comfort. What we are really looking for, but are unaware of, is a connection with the implicate order, to wholeness. The satisfaction of acquiring something will wane and eventually feel hollow, leaving us once again with a craving because it's not what we *really* wanted to begin with. These things that show up and we manifest into reality may serve good purpose by showing us what we really don't want or need, and in this way we can check them off our cosmic list. Eventually through this down-select process we'll see what gives us a true connection to wholeness, genuine satisfaction, and harmony.

As for desire, like stuff it's most likely also a teacher helping us see a clearer path to better uses of our energy and focus.

Practice Affirmation

Feed yourself good thoughts. The crow of criticism will always show up on your shoulder cawing at you when you are making important decisions. Understand that they have your best interest at heart, but they don't know you in the present tense; they don't consider your intentions and goals or know your capability, and they don't have, or care about, the complete picture. When they show up, thank them for their concern, reassure them, and then silence them.

Make a List of What You Don't Like

There's a lot of talk about finding out what you *like* but we often have no idea what that is, so we potentially set ourselves up for frustration and churn trying to find our happiness and purpose in others' opinions or feeling around in the dark. This happens in part when we listen to the ill-informed opinions of our peers instead of acting on and following our own path, doing independent research, and asking the opinions of those senior to us. The idea is to get out there and act at the same time you're listening to your friend's caring but sometimes suspect advice. There's a ton of polarized talk along the lines of exclusively pursuing the things you like, while rejecting and avoiding everything else (with prejudice). This is patently bad advice, whether it's given by society, pop culture, the uninformed, a disgruntled relative, or because you simply perceive it's a good idea to snub everything and do nothing until your purpose hits you on the head. To figure out what you want from life, start with a list of what you personally already *know* you don't like, and then look at the opposite of those things.

Build Routine and Structure

Many people today think that freedom shouldn't require things like repetition, routine, structure, effort, hard work, pain, or discomfort but the truth is there's no quicker way to get yourself enslaved to someone or something than to do nothing and give your power and control away. Freedom is an inside job. There is freedom in discipline, in strength, in structure, even in suffering, though I admittedly avoid it. While I'm not telling you to go out and flog yourself, I am saying to not avoid difficulty when it comes to call. Use it. Even the most successful creative, unstructured, undisciplined, and independent person put effort and hard work into their relaxed bliss. To them, the structures they leveraged and endured weren't cages; they were scaffolding to ascend and vehicles in which to fly. Confidence is the affirmation of a healthy structure and an important way station on the road to your hero story.

Enjoy the Ride

I hope you've enjoyed this book as much as I've enjoyed writing it! I'm not proposing one specific recipe to follow in order to live your best life and story and live an intuitive, successful unthinking life. But I am suggesting that there *is* one and you should take what I've given you and find out what that is. It's human nature to want to be "done" with things and move on, to snap a chalk line on what feels right, or complete, but life is iterative, and this doesn't apply to your story. You are *quanta*, energy. If quantum physics has taught us anything, it's that when we think we have discovered the origins of life and the universe, it's merely another appearance, an abstraction, the latest iteration of discovery, and not the end. We once thought atoms were the building blocks of life and then we discovered protons, neutrons, and quarks, only to discover new universes beyond these. We keep finding a finer constitution, and the definitive answers keep receding. Thanks for being here today, for living and being in the universe. I will leave you with the idea that ultimately your number one spiritual guide is you, as is the caretaker of your story, and this story becomes yours once you give it away.

Dr. Zabiegalski is available to talk to your organization or venue about ambidexterity research or speak informatively and eloquently about organizational culture, leadership, strategy, learning, complexity, business neuroscience, creativity, mindfulness, talent management, personal success, emotional intelligence, Action Learning, or storytelling. Contact Eric about a talk, keynote presentation, workshop, or coaching today! Zabba4@comcast.net or on LinkedIn.

Ingram Content Group UK Ltd.
Milton Keynes UK
UKHW020003010423
419497UK00008B/47